LAMBETH'S VICTORIAN ARC

Church of St John the Divine, Vassall Road by
George Edmund Street (1871-74)

EDMUND BIRD AND FIONA PRICE
PHOTOGRAPHS BY HARRY OSENI

London Borough of Lambeth and the Lambeth Local History Forum

2017

Acknowledgements

The publication of this book received generous financial support from Lambeth Planning Department in recognition of it being a definitive and authorative evidence-based resource appraising a key period in the borough's social, economic and architectural history. This resource will be used to inform planning outcomes and neighbourhood planning to ensure that new developments build upon and contribute to the borough's local distinctiveness, identity and sense of place. We are grateful to David Joyce and Doug Black, Assistant Directors of Lambeth Planning & Development, for agreeing this funding and editing assistance. The authors thank the following for permitting the use of their images (all copyright and not to be reproduced): Christine Wagg at the Peabody Trust for photo on p.110; Graham Gower for Hambly Mansions on p.139 and Streatham Methodist church on p.180; Henry Long for St Peter's Clapham interior view on p.160; St Peter's Vauxhall present-day interior image on p.149: © Light Perceptions Ltd & Lighting Design; Gavin Stamp for history and images of St Agnes Church on p.178; Tom Burnham for East Brixton station on p.184; London Transport Museum (Stockwell and Oval stations on p.205: images © TfL from the London Transport Museum); Bill Linksey for the Empress Theatre on p.209; The Theatres Trust for the Camberwell Empire on p.209; Tim Walder for advice on London Board Schools, John East for colour images on pp. 171, 172, 173, 176-78, 183, 184, 191 and 202; and Bob Speel for the photos of Southbank House on p.73 - www.speel.me.uk.

The assistance of Jon Newman, Len Reilly and Zoe Darani at Lambeth Archives and Kenneth and Margaret Bird for their help in editing the book was greatly appreciated. With thanks to the Barclays Bank archivist Andrea Waterhouse for information and historic images on their Clapham and former Streatham and Upper Norwood branches on pp.61-63; to Sally Cholewa at RBS Archives for information on NatWest branches at Herne Hill, Waterloo and West Norwood on pp.62-64; to the Jamyang Buddhist Centre for arranging the photo on p.15 and to Martin Humphries and Robert Holden at the Cinema Museum p.35.

Image left: boiler stokers at the South Metropolitan Gasworks in Vauxhall in c1900 (the site of Phoenix House and Lambeth Planning Department).

Published in 2017 by Lambeth Archives and Lambeth Local History Forum

Lambeth Archives, 52 Knatchbull Road, London SE5 9QY www.lambeth.gov.uk/Services/leisureCulture/LocalHistory/Archives
www.landmark.lambeth.gov.uk

Designed and printed by Whatever Design www.whateverdesign.co.uk (designer: Tom Ward) - ISBN 978-0-9926695-4-6

CONTENTS

Foreword by Helen Hayes MP 5

Map of the Borough in 1870 6

Introduction.. 7

Public buildings 13

Public realm and sculpture.. 21

Public libraries 23

Health.. 32

Education... 38

Parks 50

Shops 54

Banks 61

Transport 65

Industry 72

Public Houses 77

Housing 106

Churches.. 142

Lost Victorian buildings of Lambeth 170

Bibliography and sources 211

Index.. 212

More faces of Lambeth: clockwise from top left: Lambeth Football Club in 1894; West Norwood Cycling Club in c1880; schoolmistresses at the Wesleyan Day School on Eden Road in West Norwood in c1880; and a milkman on his way from Curtis Brothers Dairy (later Unigate Dairies) on Valley Road, Streatham in his delivery cart in c1900.

FOREWORD BY HELEN HAYES MP FOR DULWICH & WEST NORWOOD

In this book, the fifth in a series appraising Lambeth's architectural heritage, we dive back in time to explore the richly diverse buildings built during the reign of Queen Victoria (1837 - 1901). The face of Lambeth was transformed in this period as rapid urbanisation took hold, ranging from tightly packed terraces and tenements in the north of the borough, often cheek-by-jowl with industry and commerce, to spacious avenues of detached and semi-detached villas laid out over fields and market gardens in Brixton, Clapham, Streatham, Norwood and West Dulwich.

This was the era before town planning by local government, so development was largely the preserve of private builders and businessmen. Their projects ranged from just a handful of houses or a few residential streets to whole neighbourhoods planned by great master-builders such as Thomas Cubitt who laid out Clapham Park, and Hanney and Ellis at Telford Park in Streatham. Later in the century philanthropic organisations embarked on ambitious housing schemes for the working classes, most notably the Leigham Court Estate in Streatham, the Milkwood Estate in Herne Hill and the Peabody Estate in Waterloo. Elegant shopping districts grew up to serve the new residents and these attractive parades can still be appreciated today in West Norwood, Streatham and Brixton – they are an important and much loved part of our heritage in South London.

The catalyst for these developments was rapid investment in transport and sanitation infrastructure. In the 1830s people moved around slowly by horse-drawn carriages but by the 1870s the network of suburban railways we depend on today was established, augmented by tramways, which enabled commuters to enjoy leafy suburban living while retaining good access to the City and West End central business districts. The Victorians were passionate about improving health and well-being, and embarked on great construction projects to supply clean water and provide efficient sewage systems, building waterworks and the impressive Victoria and Albert embankments designed by the great Sir Joseph Bazalgette.

Education improved immeasurably from the mid-Victorian era as the dynamic London School Board built 'beacons of learning' throughout the capital – their legacy is still very evident today and they are highly cherished local landmarks. Towards the end of the century, municipal reform established the great London County Council which set about improving the lives of Londoners, planning progressive housing projects and laying out most of the fine public parks we enjoy today, such as Brockwell Park in my constituency.

This book charts the progress made throughout Victoria's long reign, exploring the different building types and open spaces, most of which have survived wartime destruction and post-war redevelopment, and remain for us to enjoy and treasure today. Our challenge now is how best to conserve this great legacy whilst accommodating the needs and the growth of the 21st Century, and that will require careful planning. I hope the wealth of information within this book can contribute to informing this process and we can continue the great Victorian tradition of using fine architecture and design to create new developments we, and future generations, can be equally proud of.

Helen Hayes has been the MP for Dulwich & West Norwood since 2015. Before entering Parliament Helen was a chartered town planner.

MAP OF LAMBETH IN 1870

(railways revised in 1891)

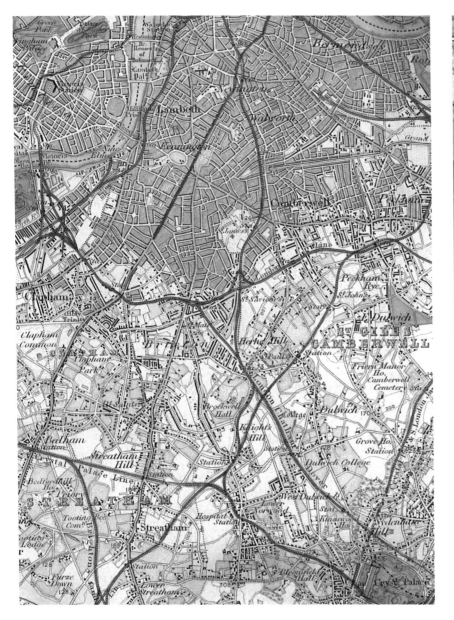

Pictured above is the Grade II listed pillar box at the junction of Mervan Road and Rattray Road in Brixton. It is a rare surviving example of the hexagonal cast iron Penfold design, named after its designer John Wornham Penfold (1828-1909). It was designed in 1866 and this one dates from 1872. They were installed throughout the British Isles and in countries within the British Empire including India, New Zealand and Australia. Note the royal cypher VR (Victoria Regina), the acanthus leaf decoration and finial mount.

INTRODUCTION

This is the fifth volume in our series on the architectural history of Lambeth. The first volume, *Lambeth's Edwardian Splendours* which appraised the period 1901-1914 was published in 2010 (revised and expanded in a second edition in 2013), followed by *Lambeth Architecture 1914-39*, published in 2012, *Lambeth Architecture 1945-65: A Brave New World* in 2014, and *Lambeth Architecture 1965-99* in 2015. Following the completion of these four volumes spanning the 20th century we now go back in time to assess the architecture of the borough which dates from the reign of Queen Victoria (1837-1901).

The Victorian era marked the transition of Lambeth from a largely rural landscape (apart from the already-built-up Waterloo and north Lambeth) to a largely urbanised one. The impact of the industrial revolution coupled with the development of transport links via rail and river on the development of London is hard to overstate. Lambeth was well-placed to benefit from these improvements, and in the later 19th century the north of the borough became one of the most densely-populated and industrialised areas in London. Between 1831 and 1891 the population of the Parish of Lambeth rose by almost 200,000 and by the end of the queen's reign in 1901 Lambeth was a very different place from the time of her accession.

Although large pockets of poverty, poor housing adjoining noxious industry and poor public health remained, particularly in the north of the parish, south of the Oval there were new neighbourhoods of middle class terraced housing with smart shopping districts large, attractive public parks and new leisure attractions, such as sports clubs and theatres.

Major new infrastructure projects such as the Albert Embankment, railway and tram services changed the face of the area, and the old local government structures were swept away and replaced by the forward-thinking and democratic London County Council and Metropolitan Borough of Lambeth, which had bold plans to transform Lambeth for the better.

The villages of Brixton, Norwood and, although not yet part of Lambeth, Clapham and Streatham, changed from being country villages to highly desirable middle class suburbs.

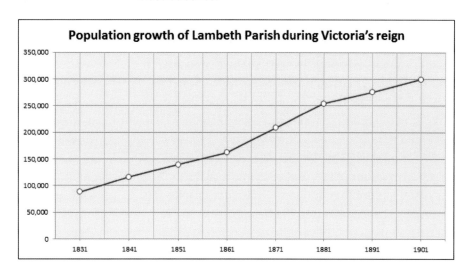

Population growth of Lambeth Parish during Victoria's reign

Market stalls on The Cut in c1872 with the Old Vic on the right.

North Lambeth and Vauxhall

Much of the north of the borough along the riverside to Nine Elms and the streets south of the river at Waterloo was in a sorry state by the mid-19th century. Industrialisation had spread up-river and the new rail links to Waterloo and Nine Elms encouraged more industry. In the 1830s between the thriving boat builders, wharves, potteries and soap factories, the poverty and over-crowding was some of the worst in London. The rapid urbanisation had many negative effects on the area and pollution, unregulated development, few regulatory powers over industry and poor public health compounded to make parts of this district unsanitary and unsavoury. Waterloo Road had a reputation for petty crime, but despite this the area's street markets in the New Cut and Lower Marsh had between them more costermongers than any other market in London. By contrast, in the 1870s

South Lambeth was a respectable and prosperous suburb with smart thoroughfares such as Lansdowne Gardens. There were numerous theatres in the north including Gattis and the Canterbury providing popular, sometimes unruly entertainment. In the 1880s Emma Cons, ran a not overly successful campaign to encourage entertainment without alcohol, through the Coffee Palace Association at the Royal Victoria Music Hall, which later became the Old Vic Theatre.

Kennington

By 1840 Kennington was characterised by ribbon development with many large houses built along the main roads towards Brixton and Clapham. The Oval cricket ground was opened in 1846 just before the peace of Kennington Common was disturbed by the Chartists march of 1848. An example of the elegance of the area was the Horns Tavern assembly rooms. But there was also industry such as a soap factory and parts of the district declined during the latter half of the century as large houses were split into multiple occupation and some properties slipped into a poor state of repair.

Brixton and Stockwell

Brixton and Stockwell were largely rural at the beginning of Victoria's reign. It was still possible to walk across the fields to Kennington, to buy strawberries in the market gardens of Myatts Fields or follow the River Effra along Brixton Road. Apart from the Trinity Almshouses and the House of Correction (now Brixton Prison) people lived largely in ignorance of the harsher conditions in the north of the parish. The opening of Vauxhall Bridge in 1816 prompted much suburban development, but even by 1880 there were very few shops other than Francis & Son, established in 1839, and Bon Marche at the corner of Ferndale Road. In 1888 Electric Avenue was established, illuminated by new electric lights generating a feeling of prosperity and progress, and cementing Brixton's position as a smart shopping centre. The largest single development was the prestigious Angell Town - large villas laid out on tree-lined avenues in the 1850s to the east of Brixton Road. The railway accelerated growth and by 1890 Brixton and Stockwell were respectable and aspirational middle class suburbs.

St Andrew's church and Hammerton's Brewery in Stockwell Green in c1910

Streatham

City merchants moved from London after the Great Fire of 1666 and attracted by Streatham Spa, established Streatham as a place of wealth and status well before the Victorian era. The population rose from 6,000 in 1841 to 21,600 in 1881 and 71,650 by 1900. Pratts Department Store opened in the 1850s and Streatham attracted wealthy people aided by coach travel into London, the coming of the railways in the 1850s and trams in 1891. Fine estates of homes were laid out such as Telford Park, Coventry Park and Leigham Court, giving rise to the development of shops and businesses along the High Road.

Norwood

Norwood remained a largely rural area throughout the earlier years of the nineteenth century. Roads were laid after the 1806 Enclosure Act, and the death of Lord Thurlow enabled land to be sold for development. The South Metropolitan Cemetery was laid out in 1837. More rapid development took place after the arrival of the railway in 1856. In 1851 the population of the district of St Luke's, Norwood, was 3,977, and there were 647 houses. By 1901 the population had increased nearly tenfold to 35,888, and there were 6,431 houses and Norwood Road was lined with shops.

Clapham

Many large houses existed around the Common in the eighteenth century – bankers and merchants had moved out of London after the Great Fire, the availability of clean air and water drawing people away from the increasingly disease-ridden and polluted inner city areas of London. Thomas Cubitt's development of the upmarket Clapham Park estate of middle class housing, contributed to a population increase of 13,500 between 1821 and 1861.

Local Government in the 19th century

The main body of local government at the start of the Victorian era was the parish or Vestry. Modern-day Lambeth comprises the ancient parish of Lambeth together with Streatham and Clapham which were added in 1965. The responsibilities of the parish grew in this period, probably the most important change came in 1855 when the vestry was required to appoint a Medical Officer of Health and an Inspector of Nuisances for the first time. Both appointments were long overdue. In 1853 a deputation headed by William Williams M.P. for Lambeth pointed out to Lord Palmerston that *"many of the inhabitants of Lambeth, suffering from the effects of bad drainage, have been compelled to leave their houses. The cellars and kitchens in numerous instances were full of water several feet deep."*

By the later 19th century boards had been established for all sorts of functions such as cemeteries and libraries. London-wide government started with the Metropolitan Board of Works from 1855 and then after 1889 the London County Council – an elected body that gave London an energetic and cohesive form of government, taking Lambeth out of Surrey after 1889. Welfare was provided through the Poor Law Boards of Guardians which ran workhouses and, by the end of the period public hospitals.

Transport and communication

The main arterial roads through Lambeth were all largely in place by the 1830s and the Metropolitan Board of Works' development of the road system, including the Albert Embankment, further enhanced communications in the borough. From the 1870s horse trams offering reliable inexpensive mass transport helped to accelerate suburbanisation. Lambeth's first [horse-drawn] tramway, travelling from Kennington to Westminster, opened in 1861. The photo below shows a cable-line 'gripper' tram on Brixton Hill in c1900. By 1846 the only stagecoach still operating from London was to Redhill and Brighton. London's first passenger railway opened between London and Greenwich in 1836 followed by the London & Southampton Railway to Woking in 1838 terminating at Nine Elms, extended to Waterloo in 1848. The "pre-industrial world" said W.M. Thackeray "has passed into limbo and vanished". Lambeth's growth further accelerated with the advent of the suburban lines in the 1850s and 1860s - by the late 1860s stations had been opened at Herne Hill, Tulse Hill, Streatham, Streatham Hill, Gipsy Hill, Brixton, Loughborough Junction and Clapham. The Underground arrived towards the end of the Victorian era with the first deep underground railway running from Stockwell to King William Street opening in 1890, extended to Clapham Common in 1900. It was to be some years before the carriages had windows!

Health and social conditions

Social conditions in Lambeth varied hugely over both time and place during this period and improvements did not take place in a consistent fashion: overcrowding was, in some places as bad at the end of the century as it had been in the 1840s. In north Lambeth the major problems were polluted water supplies and sewage disposal. Recognition of a major problem came when in 1854 John Snow discovered that diseases such as cholera could be carried by water and almost all drinking water came from the Thames. Outbreaks were recorded in 1848 and 1849 despite the Cholera Act of 1832. In Lambeth 1,618 people died from cholera in the 1849 outbreak, some of the worst fatalities of all the London districts.

Sources as early as the 1841 census and as late as Booth's poverty map of 1899 show areas of huge deprivation. George Augustus Sala writing in 1859 noted that the New Cut (The Cut today) *"isn't picturesque, it isn't quaint, it isn't curious….It is simply Low. It is sordid, squalid, and the truth must out, disreputable."* Overcrowding and insanitary housing and drainage conditions led to sewerage effluent being dumped in the Thames. Sir Samuel Peto speaking in Parliament called Lambeth *"one vast cesspool"*. According to the first annual report of Lambeth's Medical Officer of Health in 1856 at least one tenth of the inhabited houses in the Parish of Lambeth were in an *"unwholesome"* condition. The engraving of 1850 is from Gustave Dore's *London A Pilgrimage* (1872) illustrating Vauxhall Gas Works.

The Metropolis Local Management Act 1855 transferred management of local sewerage and drainage into the hands of Vestries and Boards. By 1857 8,432 feet of sewer and three new gulleys for street drainage, provided 400 more houses with drainage. 1,652ft of ditches were also filled in. The "Great Stink" of 1858 prompted Joseph Bazalgette, the Chief Engineer to the Metropolitan Board of Works since 1855, to plan the construction of major sewerage systems in the 1860s, those on the south bank of the Thames running under the Albert Embankment.

In the latter half of Victoria's reign campaigners were working to improve housing conditions for many. There were quasi-philanthropical organisations such as the Peabody Trust, who built the Stamford Street Estate, and the Artizans, Labourers and General Dwellings Company, who built the Leigham Court Estate in Streatham from 1889 and who worked to improve life for working people. Lord Rowton opened Bondway Hostel in 1891 recognising the need for cheap lodging in Lambeth. By contrast those living in the southern part of the parish had a much more comfortable existence, generally better housed, more prosperous and with easy access to clean water.

Education

Before the 1870 Education Act, which set up a system of universal state education run by school boards, education was provided by a range of organisations. Anglican and nonconformist churches ran schools, the former under the umbrella of the National School Society and the latter the British and Foreign School Society. Private education was common for middle and upper class families. For the poor, charity schools were established by campaigners such as Dr Barnardo. In 1851 Henry Beaufoy built the Lambeth Ragged School on Newport Street, Vauxhall and another ragged school was established on Prince's Road, now Black Prince Road in 1852.

In 1870 the Education Act set up a system of universal, eventually free compulsory secular state education for all children between the ages of five and ten, later extended up to thirteen. The London School Board set about its role with amazing vigour; providing tens of thousands of places for children who previously had no chance of education. Adult education also took a leap forward in the Victorian era with Morley College set up in the late 1880s. Other similar bodies included the Stockwell Educational Institute for Working Men in 1848, the Angell Town Literary & Scientific Institute in Brixton in 1862 and Stockwell Training College for Schoolmistresses in 1861.

Entertainment

The public house became an important place of entertainment during Victoria's reign – most of Lambeth's hostelries were built or rebuilt during the Victorian period, many of them also providing music hall type entertainment. Lambeth has many fine parks laid out in Victorian times. In 1877, the Metropolitan Board of Works purchased Clapham Common from its manorial owners, to be "free and uninclosed (sic) forever". Vauxhall Park was laid out in 1888, Brockwell Park in 1892 and Myatt's Fields in 1889. Public libraries were established in this period and there were seven libraries built in Lambeth between 1888 and 1893.

Throughout the whole of the Victorian period the music hall was extremely popular. Astley's on Westminster Bridge Road attracted large crowds and in 1851 the Canterbury Hall was opened nearby. Brixton become a favourite lodging place for music hall artistes such as Dan Leno. By contrast Vauxhall Gardens saw a slow decline during the middle of the century and eventually closed in 1859. Many popular Victorian theatres were established such as The Brixton Theatre, the Brixton Empress and the Metropole on Coldharbour Lane in Camberwell.

The six decades of Victoria's reign saw the greatest change to Lambeth's landscape in the whole of its history, transformed from a rural to an urban or suburban one. The change was in response to London's growth and industrialisation and was enabled by improved transport and speculative building. For Victorians living in newly-built suburbs such as Brixton, West Dulwich, Herne Hill, Norwood and Streatham, it offered a quality of life far removed from the circumstances of their neighbours living only a few miles away to the north.

PUBLIC BUILDINGS

Lambeth Vestry Hall (picture right and bottom right in c1865) now **367 Kennington Road**, was built in 1853 and served the parish and Vestry of Lambeth for nearly half a century, becoming Lambeth Town Hall when the new Metropolitan Borough was formed in 1900 until its new town hall in Brixton was completed in 1908. It became the headquarters of the Church of England Children's Society and later the British Field Sports Society and the Countryside Alliance. It is a dignified classical composition with a tetrastyle (four columned) Tuscan portico, modillion cornice and pediment, occupying an island site in the heart of Kennington. It is a Grade II listed building.

The **former London County Council (LCC) Weights and Measures office** at **43 Netherford Road**, Clapham (below left) was built at the very end of Queen Victoria's reign in 1901. Grade II listed, it exhibits a delightful 'streaky bacon style' (red brick and string courses of white Portland stone), with Arts and Crafts detailing to the leaded windows and the pair of flamboyant porches, one of which is inscribed 'LCC'.

The former Gipsy Hill Police Station (top photo) dates from 1854 and served Upper Norwood until a new police station was built nearby on Central Hill in 1939 (see entry in *Lambeth Architecture 1914-39*). It was converted to police flats in 1948 and is now simply **10 Gipsy Hill**.

It was designed by Charles Reeves (1815-66) Surveyor to the Metropolitan Police from 1843 who completed over 40 police stations in the capital. It has a most attractive façade of yellow brick with rusticated quoins, piers and central entrance portal, its fine sash windows surviving intact.

Cavendish Road Police Station was built in 1891 and designed by John Butler (1828-1900), who was Surveyor to the Metropolitan Police from 1881 to 1895 when he was succeeded by his son John Dixon Butler. It resembles a late-Victorian villa with red brick vernacular elevations, homely canted bay window and hipped slate roof with red ridge tiles. It is set back behind a front garden, only the classical entrance portal and blue lamp indicating its use. To the rear is a more substantial and plainer yellow and red brick three-storey block.

Renfrew Road Magistrates' Court (now the **Jamyang Buddhist Centre**) in Kennington is a charming Grade II listed building, built in 1869 and designed by Thomas Charles Sorby (1836-1924) who was the Metropolitan Police Surveyor at the time. It is of red brick in Flemish bond with stone dressings and a slate roof, designed in a picturesque Free Tudor style.

It served as a Police Court for nearly 100 years (middle photo: 1955), closing in c1969 when the new Camberwell Green Magistrates' Courts opened. It became a maximum security court for special remands, often featuring on the television news in the late 1960s, 1970s and 1980s. The Court served a number of high profile trials including the Kray Twins in 1968, the armed gang involved in the Iranian Embassy siege of 1980 and numerous IRA terrorists. It finally closed in 1990 and was used for filming an episode of the TV series "The Bill". Thereafter, the building fell into disrepair.

It was listed Grade II in 1993 and in 1995 it was rescued by the Buddhist community who then worked with Lambeth's conservation officer and English Heritage on a scheme to convert the building to a new place of worship. The cells were transformed into bedrooms, the court room became the principal prayer room and the high-security walled courtyard and the old legal library are now occupied by a cafe with a golden statue of the Parinirvana Buddha in the courtyard garden. The magistrates' dining room is now a smaller temple.

It is one of an important group of historic civic buildings sitting between the former fire station and the former Lambeth Workhouse later the Lambeth Hospital (see pages 17 and 34) and opposite the Police Section House of 1938.

Lambeth has a trio of fine mid-Victorian fire stations dating from the 1860s, all superseded by later and larger replacements. The **former Clapham Fire Station** on **The Polygon** (top photo) was built in 1868 and designed by Edward Cresy Junior (1824-70), architect to the Metropolitan Board of Works and the London Fire Brigade. This Grade II listed building (now a house) was built in the Gothic style comprising polychrome brickwork, stock brick in Flemish bond and a slate roof with four chimney stacks. It is seen in the middle photo in 1869 soon after it opened with a pair of horse-drawn fire engines and a telescopic ladder. After only 33 years in service it was replaced by a new fire station on the Old Town in 1902, in turn replaced in 1964.

The **former Brixton Fire Station, 240 Ferndale Road** built in c1867 has been restored as part of Squire and Partners' new office scheme (bottom left photo). The locally listed building is pictured below in c1905 with two horse-drawn engines and the firemen resplendent in their full uniform, local boys posing on the ladder. It closed when the current larger fire station opened on Gresham Road in 1904. The arcaded ground floor was lost many years ago but was reinstated in 2017.

A Turn Out. Old Brixton L.F.B.

The **Old Fire Station** on **Renfrew Road** in Kennington was built in two phases - the earlier part (seen in the foreground in the top photo and the middle photo taken in c1880) was also designed by Edward Cresy and built in 1868. It is of stock brick with red brick dressings, its watch tower survives to the rear - an essential part of the fire service before the advent of the telephone, it enabled fires to be spotted from an elevated level and the brigade dispatched. The appliance bays were adapted to windows when the larger Jacobean-style extension was opened in 1896. Designed by London County Council architect Robert Pearsell, the expanded complex included a recreation room, first floor dormitory for single firemen, flats for married officers and stables to the rear. Listed Grade II in 2000, it is now flats.

The **former West Norwood Fire Station**, **24 Norwood High Street**, (bottom photos, right hand view c1900) opened in 1881. The four-storey Gothic-style red brick building with watch tower behind served the community until a replacement opened on Norwood Road in 1914. Home to the popular South London Theatre since 1967, it is a Grade II listed building.

London has many charming post office delivery and sorting offices dating back over a century. **Brixton Royal Mail delivery office** at **20 Blenheim Gardens** is a delight. Built in 1891 and designed in the Queen Anne style, it has an imposing giant pediment with gloriously decorated patterned brickwork and below that, as a centrepiece, Queen Victoria's crown and insignia and the date of construction. Two segmental pediments preside over the entrances (one now blocked). This grand façade fronts a simple single-storey slated dual pitched roofed structure behind. It is locally listed.

On a parallel street to the south of Blenheim Gardens is **Brixton Waterworks**, appropriately located on **Waterworks Road**. The reservoir was built on a 16 acre site by the Lambeth Waterworks Company in 1834, the buildings following by 1852. They are one- and two-storey structures of yellow stock brick and slate roofs, arranged informally across the large site. The former Engineers' Office on Waterworks Road has a formal classical stone frontage bay added in the 1900s (middle photo). In 1937 a pumping station was built on Jebb Avenue (see *Lambeth architecture 1914-39*).

Streatham Pumping Station is a playful architectural triumph in the Moorish style. This Grade II* listed building was built on **Conyers Road** in 1888. It has a two-storey tower with angle turrets topped by a copper dome with a finial. At the southern end is a porch set within a half-domed apsidal projection. Attached to the north of the tower is a circular structure and a circular entrance porch, both also with domes. It was built by the Southwark and Vauxhall Water Company which was created following a merger in 1843. Both water companies were taken over by the Metropolitan Water Board in 1903.

Longfield Hall on **Knatchbull Road** (top photo) was gifted by William Minet who presented Myatt's Fields Park to the residents of West Camberwell. The Grade II listed building was built in 1889 as the parish hall for the nearby Church of St James. Elegantly detailed in yellow stock and red brick with stone dressings, its conical ended roof is particularly notable. It is a rehearsal and performance space and is hired for community events.

The **Wheatsheaf Hall** off **South Lambeth Road** (middle photo) was built in 1896 as a Congregational Church mission hall and a church lending library. The design exhibits a Tudor influence with elevations of red brick with stone dressings. The front block has an apsidal ended roof and a picturesque turret with a ribbed stone conical roof set behind. The hall was bought by Lambeth Council in 1946 and let out. It was listed Grade II in 1975 and in 1988 it was converted into a community centre.

The **Raleigh Workshop** at **1A Saltoun Road** in Brixton was built as the Effra Public Hall in 1885 (bottom photo and engraving of 1885). Once part of Raleigh Hall (now the Black Cultural Archives), it was occupied by the Brixton Liberal Club, then a private school and in recent years, a furniture workshop. It has a fine and well-restored façade of stock brick with red brick dressings.

The **Oval cricket ground** at Kennington has been the home of the Surrey County Cricket Club since 1845, also hosting the first football cup final in 1872 and early international football games. Spectators sat on the lawns under trees before this pavilion was built in 1898. It was designed by A.T. Muirhead (who also designed the pavilion at Lancashire's cricket ground at Old Trafford). The six-storey red brick locally listed pavilion was enhanced in 2013 by the addition of a new stone-columned portico designed by Adam Architecture.

At the busy road junction at **Kennington Cross** is a well preserved Grade II listed late-Victorian **underground gentlemen's public convenience** built in 1898. It closed in 1988 and stood disused until it was transformed into the ArtsLav exhibition and performance gallery in 2003.

It retains its white tiled walls, 10 urinal stalls with white porcelain bases and black marble modesty screens, mosaic floor, wood-panelled attendant's kiosk and high level cast iron glazed cistern. At street level, elaborate ornamental cast iron railings enclose the steps and a 20 foot high ventilation column and a stone cattle trough with lower dog trough complete this fine ensemble.

PUBLIC REALM AND SCULPTURE

The **South Bank Lion** has stood proudly on its granite plinth at the gateway to Lambeth on **Westminster Bridge** next to County Hall since 1966. This is its third home - originally it stood atop the Lion Brewery erected in 1837 (see entry on page 181). When this was demolished to make way for the Royal Festival Hall in the late 1940s it was painted red and moved beside the entrance to the Festival of Britain near Waterloo Station, unveiled in 1951. Grade II* listed, it is made of Coade stone, a ceramic stoneware perfected by the Lambeth artificial stone entrepreneur, Eleanor Coade in c1770.

The Grade II listed Gothic revival-style **Dyce Drinking Fountain** on **Streatham Green** (middle left photo) was erected in 1862 to commemorate the artist William Dyce in gratitude for his work on the nearby St Leonard's Church. The **ventilation pipe** and lamps (left), which once served public lavatories below, stands on **Binfield Road** near Stockwell station, it was erected in c1900. The bottom photos are of two **Victorian stone troughs** erected by the Metropolitan Drinking Fountain and Cattle Trough Association, on **Clapham Common** (1877, locally listed, left) and **Streatham Common** (1880, Grade II listed).

The Albert Embankment was constructed between 1866 and 1869, it was completed eight months before its sister the Victoria Embankment opened in 1870. Together they represent perhaps the finest engineering feat in London of the Victorian era. Both were designed by the renowned Sir Joseph Bazalgette (1819-91) who was the chief engineer to the Metropolitan Board of Works between 1856 and 1889. The Grade II listed structure extends for nearly one mile (1.5km) between Vauxhall Bridge and Westminster Bridge. The promenade behind the granite wall is lined with cast iron lamp standards, their bases formed of interlinked sturgeons (popularly known as dolphins), wreathed columns and globe lanterns, the plinths facing the river bear a bronze lion head with a ring in its mouth. Benches on raised platforms afford views across the river to Westminster, they have elaborate end supports in the shape of swans. The photos below show the Albert Embankment under construction in 1866 (top left), looking north from Lambeth Bridge in c1938 (bottom left) and a view today towards Westminster Bridge.

PUBLIC LIBRARIES

The five years between 1888 and 1893 saw an impressive total of seven new libraries opening in what is the modern day Lambeth. This was the result of a majority vote in 1886 by residents to adopt the Public Libraries Act of 1850 and establish free libraries.

The Tate Library South Lambeth, 180 South Lambeth Road opened in 1888, a gift of the sugar magnate and philanthropist Sir Henry Tate. It was designed by his appointed architect Sydney R.J. Smith (1858-1913) who went on to design the Tate Gallery on Millbank of 1897. It is a handsome locally listed three-storey red brick edifice with an elaborate stone pediment above the corner entrance bay. As the bottom left photo taken in 1931 shows, the building originally sported a magnificent pair of cupolas and a prow-ended entrance porch supported by stone caryatids (female figures), sadly demolished in the 1960s. Their reinstatement would greatly benefit this locally listed landmark. The bottom photo, also taken in 1931, shows the reading room.

The original **West Norwood Library, 14-16 Knight's Hill** was also designed by Sidney R.J. Smith and opened in 1888. Its Flemish-style façade is of red brick, terracotta and Ham Hillstone dressings and panels of roughcast render. The central two-storey loggia has an elaborate swan's neck pediment with the date 1887 in carved brick. The first-floor balcony has seven tapering fluted piers bearing busts of Homer, Sir Walter Scott, Chaucer, Shakespeare, Milton, Dickens and Socrates. It is Grade II listed. The library closed in 1969 when its replacement opened on a site opposite. It then became a community centre, hosting the library again when the 1969 building closed suddenly in 2010 after its roof was stripped by thieves and it flooded. Below: the artist's perspective and ground floor plan of 1887 and the children's library in c1938.

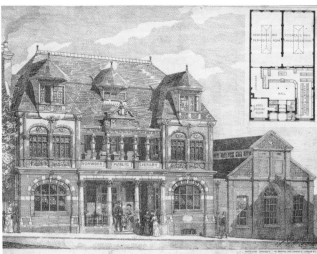

The **Durning Library, 167 Kennington Lane** was opened in 1889, Lambeth's third library to be designed by Sydney R.J. Smith. It was named after a Miss J. Durning Smith who provided the site and building **at a** cost of about £10,000. The tall façade is incredibly elaborate, described in the Historic England listing entry as *'Gothic Revival with North Italian and Flemish attributes'*. It has a projecting open arcaded ground floor, a second-floor loggia, and a highly decorated gable below which rests a sculpture of a griffin. The tower is crowned by a steep pyramidal roof with half-timbered detailing. The illustration below is from the Builder published in 1888, the photo of the interior dates from c1931.

The original **Clapham Library, 1 Clapham Common Northside** opened in 1889 in what was then part of Wandsworth. It served the community for 123 years until it closed in 2012 to be replaced by a new library on Clapham High Street. The building was designed by Edward B. l'Anson (1843-1912) who was born in Clapham and trained under Alfred Waterhouse, architect of the Natural History Museum and Manchester Town Hall.

l'Anson also designed the Clapham School of Art on Edgeley Road (1885), Newington Library (1891) and the public baths on Manor Place (1895), both in Walworth. Clapham Library was opened by Sir John Lubbock, Vice-chairman of the LCC. It originally had on the ground floor a large reading room, reference library and closed bookstacks holding 27,000 volumes. Books were retrieved by the librarians on request (see plan below). The building was converted to a new community arts centre - the **Clapham Omnibus** - which opened in 2013.

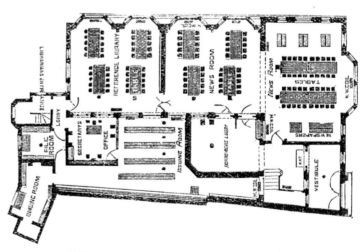

CLAPHAM PUBLIC LIBRARY, GROUND FLOOR.

Streatham Tate Library, 63 Streatham High Road (in Wandsworth until 1965) was opened in 1891 and has served the community ever since. It too was designed by Sidney R.J. Smith, commissioned by Streatham parish and funded by Sir Henry Tate, who lived at the nearby Park Hill mansion. It is a classical building of Portland stone with a copper-domed cupola. Rectangular in plan, its central entrance vestibule below the dome led into a newspaper and periodicals room to the north, a magazine room to the south and a lending library to the east. A staircase with iron stick balusters leads down to the basement and up to the first-floor rooms.

The clock was added in 1912 and the entrance was moved to Pinfold Road when the building was refurbished in 2014. After many years and great perseverance, the Streatham Society finally convinced Historic England to list the building Grade II in 2016. The perspective and ground floor plan dates from 1890 and the top view from 1948.

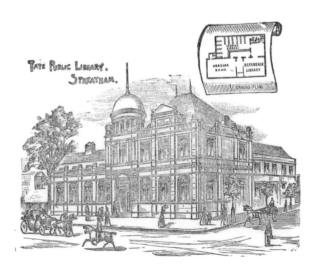

Brixton Tate Library on **Brixton Oval** is Lambeth's central lending and reference library. It was also endowed by Sir Henry Tate and designed by Sydney R.J. Smith, and was opened by the Prince of Wales (later King Edward VII) in 1893 (seen arriving in the bottom left photo). The Free Renaissance-style façade is of Elham Valley red brick with Portland and Beer stone dressings. The Grade II listed building is a symmetrical composition with three bays of rusticated brick on a stone plinth either side of the entrance beneath a central pedimented bay, which is topped by a modest timber cupola. Inside, a grand staircase with an iron balustrade links the inner vestibule with the first floor reference library, which extends the full width of the building.

The original layout on the ground floor comprised a newspaper room to the south, a magazine room to the north and the lending library to the rear. The bottom right photo shows the public queuing up to be served at the issue desk in c1902.

APPLYING FOR BOOKS AT A FREE LIBRARY (BRIXTON).

Top photos: Brixton Library in 1897: the first floor reading room and the main issue desk.

Middle photos: the library in c1930 and c1950.

Bottom photo: Photo taken in c1905 from Tate Library Gardens, the bust of Sir Henry Tate is on a stone pedestal-plinth in the foreground (listed Grade II) and the domed tower of Brixton Theatre is on the left, it was demolished after damage in the Second World War - see page 208.

The former **North Lambeth Free Library, 14 Baylis Road**, Waterloo was built in 1893. It was the fifth public library in Lambeth to open and was inaugurated by Queen Victoria's third daughter Princess Christian of Schleswig Holstein. It is a late-Victorian Jacobean style to a design by architect J.E. Trollope with steep gables, large stone-framed window openings and an imposing arched entrance porch. To the rear is a substantial formerly double-height reading room, now floored over but with its fine roof structure exposed.

The bottom photo on this page and top left photo on the facing page show the grand reading room in 1903. The top right view of the exterior on the facing page was taken in c1960 with Lower Marsh market traders' barrows in the foreground. The library closed in 1967, moving to a smaller prefabricated building on Lower Marsh. This was rebuilt in 2001 and then the library was relocated again in 2016, to the Oasis Centre on Kennington Road.

The Victorian library building lay vacant and deteriorating until it was rescued and refurbished in the 1970s by local groups to house the Waterloo Action Centre. In 1973 the building found a new lease of life hosting community meetings, art, fitness and dance classes, and as a local advice centre. It is locally listed.

The last library to be built in Lambeth during the reign of Queen Victoria is **Upper Norwood Library, 39-41 Westow Hill** which opened in 1900. It occupies a prominent site on the corner of Beardell Street and

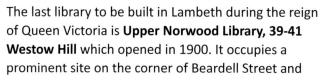

is a pleasant Victorian vernacular design by architect Edward Haslehurst in red brick with a single gable on each street frontage above pairs of large arched windows. These frame a canted corner entrance bay with arched doorway. Its pioneering 'open-access' library layout allowed the public to browse amongst the books rather than having to request them from a librarian who then had to retrieve them from 'closed-access' bookstacks.

It was built for the Library Commissioners of Lambeth and Croydon and was jointly administered by the two boroughs until 2015 when it passed solely to Lambeth. A children's library was opened within the building in 1929, replaced by a purpose-built extension in 1936 on the Beardell Street frontage, a classical-style design with a central pediment. The library was extended again with a two-storey side extension in 1965.

HEALTH

London   St. Thomas's Hospital.

St Thomas' Hospital, Lambeth Palace Road occupies a commanding site on the River Thames opposite the Houses of Parliament. Grade II listed, it was built in 1868-71 to a design by Henry Currey, who was the hospital's own architect and surveyor. The style is Italianate with some French Renaissance detailing. It is built of Fareham brick with stone dressings and slate roofs. The hospital's riverside frontage was originally a 1,666 foot (over 500 metres) long composition comprising a central entrance block (with a chapel at first-floor level) flanked by two- and three-storey wings linked by long corridors to the three four-storey pavilion blocks either side with landscaped courtyards in between (see top photo taken in c1905). An L-shaped freestanding administration building stood at the northern end fronting Westminster Bridge Road.

At the southern end is Block 9 and its Italianate campanile (photo left). This was the Medical School and also accommodated the mortuary which had a lift down to a tunnel running the length of the site along which the deceased were taken. It still exists today. In 1904 the 'Wrenaissance-style' Governors' Hall and committee room block was added in the central courtyard (see entry in *Lambeth's Edwardian Splendours*). Two blocks were added to the east in the interwar years - St Thomas' House (1925) and Riddell House nurses home designed by Sir Edwin Cooper (1937), the latter demolished in 2002 to make way for the new Evelina Children's Hospital block designed by Hopkins Architects (2005).

The Colonade.
J. Hopkins & Co., 217 Westminster Bridge Rd. S. E.   St. Thomas Hospital.

CHRISTIAN WARD, ST. THOMAS'S HOSPITAL. COPYRIGHT OF THE ARTISTIC PHOTOGRAPHIC CO., LTD., 63, BAKER STREET, W.

The hospital had 588 beds in the six pavilions - each ward having 28 beds. This design originated in France and maximised natural light and cross-ventilation, virtues promoted in England by Florence Nightingale. Historic England described St Thomas' as *'the grandest and most lavish of the English pavilion-plan hospitals, a bold and ambitious architectural set piece'* when it listed the South Wing in 2008. The matching North Wing was sadly demolished in the 1960s (it had suffered major damage in bombing raids during the Second World War but had been patched up in the 1940s) and replaced by new blocks designed by YRM architects, finished in 1976 (see *Lambeth Architecture 1965-99*). Top and middle photos: 1905. The image below is of one of a number of the ceramic tile nursery rhyme panels made by Doulton & Co. in 1896.

Puss in Boots

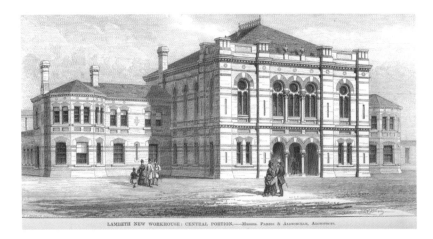

LAMBETH NEW WORKHOUSE: CENTRAL PORTION.—Messrs. Parris & Aldwinckle, Architects.

The **former Lambeth Workhouse** on **Renfrew Road** in Kennington was built in 1871, to designs by architects R. Parris and Thomas Aldwinckle. Intended to house 820 inmates (see middle left image of elderly women in the workroom in 1893), it augmented the original workhouse of 1726 on Princes Road (renamed Black Prince Road in 1939), which continued in use and was rebuilt in 1887, also by Aldwinckle. In 1876 the Lambeth Infirmary was built on Brook Drive, next to the Renfrew Road site (see photo middle right in 1966). In 1922 the workhouse and infirmary became the **Lambeth Hospital**, taken over by the LCC in 1930, who added a nurses home in 1936 and a maternity wing in 1938. By 1939 it could accommodate 1,250 patients.

The hospital passed to the National Health Service in 1948 but in 1976 the hospital was closed and patients transferred to the new North Wing at St Thomas' (see previous entry). The administrative block and chapel at the centre of the Lambeth Infirmary (seen in the top image of 1874 and bottom photo) and its lower wings (which once housed the Master of the Workhouse and his family) were originally flanked by pairs of pavilion wings linked by a long corridor but these were demolished between the 1930s and the 1980s (see plan in the Lost Lambeth chapter on page 191).

The imposing façade of the surviving central block (seen in the top left photo in 1966) is in an ornate Venetian Gothic style with polychromatic brickwork, stone dressings and dog-tooth courses of red brickwork. The central bay has a triple-arched recessed porch with carved stone capitals (bottom right photo). The central corridor has rooms either side including the former committee room, staircases at either end leading up to a large open-plan chapel which retains its magnificent hammer beam roof (see bottom left photo). The most famous inmate was the actor Charlie Chaplin who stayed there with his mother in 1896 when he was seven years old and his father had fallen into debt. The building has been home to the Cinema Museum (see top right photo) since 1998 and was eventually listed Grade II by English Heritage in 2008 after a previous listing bid was rejected in 2002.

Adjoining the central block (also known as The Master's House) is a tall water tower designed by Fowler and Hill. Also Grade II listed, it was built in 1877 to serve both the workhouse and the adjacent infirmary, combined in 1922 to form the Lambeth Hospital. It is a monumental structure echoing the Venetian Gothic style of the Master's House, built of yellow stock brick with red brick and Portland stone dressings. The large iron tank at the top (which held 38,000 gallons of water) has a hipped tiled roof with a gablet (a small ornamental gable). It is pictured left in 1966 and below after its conversion to a dwelling in 2012. Bottom left photo - one of the pair of attractive locally listed workhouse lodges and reception blocks.

Lambeth Hospital on **Landor Road** in Stockwell largely dates from the 1990s (see *Lambeth Architecture 1965-99*) but it does retain a handful of Victorian buildings that once formed part of the **South Western Fever Hospital** founded in 1871. This comprised two separate hospital complexes, one treating smallpox and the other intended for other infectious diseases such as typhus, typhoid and scarlet fever. The surviving heritage assets include Landor House, the lodge and the two locally listed Portland stone gate piers, all seen in the top photo. See also the entry in Lost Lambeth chapter on page 191.

The public dispensary was an important part of healthcare provision in Britain before the advent of the National Insurance Act of 1911. A network of both private and charitable dispensaries developed rapidly in Victorian London, primarily for less wealthy citizens who could not afford the fees of a doctor. They were outpatient institutions with physicians in attendance at certain times and dispensing chemists who also gave treatment advice.

Two examples of dispensaries are pictured here - the middle image is of the former **Stockwell and North Brixton Dispensary** at **44-46 Wilkinson Street** off Albert Square in South Lambeth (locally listed) - a fine Venetian Gothic-style building of 1866 with polychromatic brickwork, arch headed windows and a grand Gothic porch with composite columns. **42 Clapham Manor Street** (bottom photo - Grade II listed) was purpose-built as the **Clapham Dispensary** in 1854. Designed by J.T. Knowles Senior, it is a splendid two-storey Italianate edifice of grey brick with red brick and stucco dressings including moulded architraves and keystones.

EDUCATION

Lambeth has a great wealth of school buildings erected in the Victorian era by charitable bodies, churches, private foundations and, in the second half of the queen's reign, the London School Board, created in 1870.

The **former Stockwell Educational Institute, 1 Stockwell Green** (top photo) was funded by the Stockwell New Chapel, opening in 1848 to host lectures, classes and meetings. This Grade II listed building has a handsome symmetrical Jacobean façade comprising three projecting full-height bays with leaded diamond-pane windows and a lofty central entrance portal flanked by two lower arched doorways with Doric columns. It fell into disuse in the 1970s but was subsequently restored.

Elderwood Place on **Elder Road** in Norwood was built in 1850 (photo below left) in what was then a semi-rural area. It formed part of the **Lambeth New Schools**, also known as the 'House of Industry for the Infant Poor'. Thought to be the first Poor Law (workhouse system) school in England, the institution had been established in

1810 by the Lambeth Parish Poor Law adminstrators (see entry on page 34). It is a long two-storey range with plain stock brick elevations and sash windows set within stucco-lined reveals with gauged brick arches over. In 1887 a semi-circular pedimented hood on free-standing Tuscan columns sheltering the main entrance was added (photo bottom left). The lodge (**62A Elder Road**) added in this year by Sydney R.J. Smith is particularly charming (photo below right). Following the abolition of the workhouse system in 1929 the building became a rest home and then flats. Both are Grade II listed. See also entry on page 194.

Lambeth Ragged School, 22 Newport Street, was built in 1851 for 400 poor children (the name of the school originating from their ragged appearance) by Henry Benjamin Hanbury Beaufoy (owner of the vinegar distillery that is now Regent's Bridge Gardens) as a memorial to his wife. Ragged schools were built across Britain, teaching basic literacy and trade skills such as shoe repair and tailoring.

The top image shows the complete building soon after it opened (note the railway viaduct of 1848 in the background). The classical pedimented central and north wings were demolished in 1904 to widen the railway into the Waterloo terminus. The images left and below, published in the Illustrated London News in 1846, show classrooms within. The surviving south wing is now the Beaconsfield art gallery and cafe (bottom left).

THE ILLUSTRATED LONDON NEWS.

THE LAMBETH "RAGGED SCHOOL."—(GIRLS).

The Grade II listed former **St John's School** on **Canterbury Crescent** in the heart of Brixton (top two photos, the first dating from c1910) was built to the designs of Benjamin Ferrey in 1853 to accommodate 180 boys, 120 girls and 100 infants. It is in an informal Tudor style with high pitched slated roofs, tall chimneys and red Rochester brick elevations embellished with Bath stone quoins and dressings. Damaged during World War II, it was repaired and reopened in 1947. It closed in the late 1960s and was converted to residential use.

The frontage block of **St Martin's-in-the-Fields High School for Girls, 155 Tulse Hill** was built as a villa in 1857 by Edward Groves and called Berry House, later renamed Silwood House (bottom left). It was bought by the governors of the school (founded in 1699) in 1912 and a large neo-Georgian wing added before the school transferred here from Charing Cross Road in 1928. It was opened by the Duchess of York, later the Queen Mother (photo below). This fine Grade II listed Italianate villa is stucco fronted with a grand porch at raised ground-floor level and Corinthian columns flanking the niche above.

The **Jewish Orphanage** relocated to Norwood from Stepney in 1861. Only the charming locally listed Jacobean-style lodge just off Knight's Hill on what is now **Devane Way** (top photo) survived the tragic demolition in 1961 of the magnificent 1860s buildings by Tillot and Chamberlain (see the entry in the Lost Lambeth chapter on p.187). It has cheerful red brick elevations with decorative diaper patterned dark brickwork, shaped gables, elegant porch and tall chimneys.

The **former St Peter's Parish School** and **St Peter's Orphanage and Training College** (now Herbert House) stand adjacent to the Church of St Peter on **Kennington Lane**. All were designed by J.L. Pearson (1817-97), built in 1860-64 in the Victorian Gothic style and are Grade II* listed. The three-storey Herbert House (now flats) seen left and in the

far left photo of c1912, was built for orphaned daughters of the clergy and professional families. It has elevations of stock brick with bands and dressings of Bath stone.

The former school (also now flats, photo below) on **St Oswald's Place**, behind the church, shares the same palette of materials in a similar

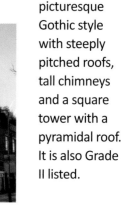

picturesque Gothic style with steeply pitched roofs, tall chimneys and a square tower with a pyramidal roof. It is also Grade II listed.

The Angell Town Literary & Scientific Institution for Working Men (now the **Karibu Education Centre**), **7 Gresham Road** in Brixton opened in 1862. By the 1890s it was the Gresham Hall and then an early telephone exchange before the present one opened to the east in the 1930s. The locally listed building (top photo) has an imposing gabled façade of stucco adorned with pediments and festoons, with a rusticated ground floor.

St Saviour's Church of England Primary School on **Herne Hill Road** was built in 1868 (middle photo). It is a single-storey building of ragstone dressed with Bath stone with Gothic pointed arch windows and five gable ends facing the front playground. It was formerly hidden from the street by the large Church of St Saviour built a year earlier in 1867, but this fine landmark was demolished in 1981 (see Lost Lambeth p. 174).

The former **St Andrew's & St John's Church of England Primary School, 74 Roupell Street** (bottom photos: 1969 and 2016) was built in c1868 (now the **EF Language Centre**). Designed by the church architect S.S. Teulon, this three-storey Grade II listed building has a U-shaped plan and is of stock brick with dressing of stone and red brick. Immediately to the north, also by Teulon is St Andrew's House, former vicarage to St John's, Waterloo.

The former **Immanuel Infants' School, 72 Colmer Road** in Streatham, dates from 1869 and is an early work by Sir Ernest George (1839-1922), president of Royal Institute of British Architects 1908-10. He designed many fine Victorian and Edwardian houses and Southwark Bridge (1921). For 50 years from the 1930s, the first floor was the headquarters of the 92nd London Company of the Boys' Brigade. It was later converted into the **Shree Swaminarayan temple**. The top photo shows it in c1980, sadly it later lost the conical roof of its elegant circular tower (see recent middle photo) - its reinstatement would be very welcome. The school master's cottages are to the left of the tower with the two-storey school room block with the gable on its right, all in stock brick with stone dressings. It is locally listed.

St Mary's Infants' School on **Lambeth Road** (later Holy Trinity Primary Infants and now **Fairley House School** - bottom right photo) was built in 1880 on land given by the then Archbishop of Canterbury Archibald Tait. It is a picturesque design in the Gothic style with two-storey gabled bays at each end and a long, low middle section with a very high and steeply pitched roof and deep, swept eaves. The Gothic stone-dressed windows are paired or grouped. It is Grade II listed. The drawing below is by Kate E. Thorpe, dated 1965.

The **School Board for London** (also known as the **London School Board** - LSB) was created under the 1870 Education Act. It was one of the first directly elected bodies with powers across the capital, each district returning four to seven members elected by secret ballot - the first time this process was used in Britain. Another first was that women could both vote and be elected to the Board. A by-law passed in 1871 required all children to attend school between the ages of five and thirteen. The Board (hence the term Board Schools) built over 400 schools throughout what is now Inner London. They were designed by its first chief architect Edward Robert Robson (1836-1917) or his assistant Thomas Jerram Bailey (1843-1910) who took over from Robson in 1885 until the LSB was abolished in 1904 when its responsibilities were transferred to the LCC. From the outset the LSB adopted a highly distinctive and attractive architectural style which represented an eclectic mix of Queen Anne, classical, Flemish, French Renaissance, Tudor Revival and later Arts and Crafts influences. Their elevations are of stock brick with red brick dressings. The steeply pitched clay tiled roofs incorporated gables, dormers, belfries, spires and/or cupolas. Most were three-storey, known as triple-deckers and therefore stood tall and proud in their settings above lower terraced housing. Infants, boys and girls were taught separately – usually infants on the ground floor, girls on the middle floor and boys on the top floor (with separate school entrances). These schools represent an exceptional social achievement and a great architectural and historical legacy and most are still in their original use.

The first three schools built in Lambeth by the LSB are pictured here. The top view is of **Wyvil Primary School** (originally called **South Lambeth Road School**), **Wyvil Road**, designed by E.R. Robson to hold 828 pupils. It was opened in 1876 and extended by T.J. Bailey in 1906. The middle view is of **Stockwell Primary, Stockwell Road**, built by Robson for 824 pupils in 1877 and extended in 1884 and 1902 (by T.J. Bailey) and again in 2012. **Lark Hall Primary School, Gaskell Street** (bottom view) in Clapham (1877) has an asymmetrical gabled façade because the intended north bay was never built. All three schools are locally listed.

Kingswood Primary is on two sites on **Gipsy Road** in Norwood. The Upper Site is Grade II listed (top photo). It was designed by Robson to accommodate 600 children, opening in 1875. It was extended in 1896 by Bailey. It has five stone-capped gabled bays to the three-storey façade, built of stock brick with dressings of red brick and Portland stone. The high pitched tiled roof has tall chimney stacks with a beautiful onion dome and weather vane. A large stone plaque on a corner elevation proudly displays its original name - **Gipsy Road Schools**. The Lower Site (originally **Salters Hill Schools**) by Robson opened in 1880 and was extended by Bailey in 1905. It has a handsome tower with an ogee cupola, and a very extensive range of attractive gabled buildings.

Clapham Manor School (originally known as **Wirtemberg Street Schools**, seen in the middle view) was built in 1881 and was also designed by Robson. It is a fine triple-decker with tall classrooms lit by large multi-pane windows, its steeply pitched tiled roofs having long gabled dormers in the Arts and Crafts tradition and oval windows with fancy cobweb style glazing on the top floor. It was extended with a new block with multi-coloured glazing by dRMM architects in 2009.

The Durand Academy in Stockwell (bottom photo) was originally two different schools, both designed by Bailey. **Hackford Road Elementary School** (by the 1950s known as Kennington Secondary School) was built for 996 pupils and opened in 1887, the south wing was added in 1894. Durand Primary School on Durand Gardens was erected in 1888 as a Pupil Teachers' school, renamed **Brixton Central School** in 1913. They later merged to create one primary school. It is locally listed as is the house built for the caretaker. The James Bond actor Roger Moore was a pupil here in the 1930s.

The locally listed former **Priory Primary and Secondary Schools** on **Priory Grove** in Stockwell (top photo) was built by Robson in 1886 for 1,200 children. Following its closure it was converted into flats in c1996.

Heathbrook Primary (originally **St Andrew's Street Schools**) on **St Rule Street**, off Wandsworth Road (1886 - middle left view) is a fine Queen Anne-style H-plan design by Bailey with a central cupola (locally listed).

Walnut Tree Walk Primary School in Kennington (bottom left) was built in 1875 and remodelled in 1907; it is a classic triple-decker with well detailed elevations and a lively roofscape of gabled dormers.

The former **Ashby Mill Primary School** in Brixton (photo left) was originally named **Lyham Road Schools** then **Parkside Primary and Secondary School**. Built in 1875, it was remodelled in 1913. The class photograph was taken in c1930. Locally listed, it was converted to flats (called **Park Lofts**) after the school closed in 1997.

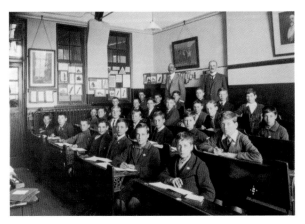

Haselrigge Junior School on **St Luke's Avenue** in Clapham (top view) was built in 1887 and extended in 1891-93 (architect T.J. Bailey) on a truly monumental scale. It is three to six storeys in height in the Queen Anne revival style. The taller central block has very large windows and is topped by a lantern with a spirelet. The ends of the wings have hipped roofs and tall gabled oriel dormers with shell hoods. It is listed Grade II and was converted to flats in 2005, renamed **Reed Place**.

Hill Mead Primary School on **Moorland Road** in Brixton (bottom left view) was designed by Bailey and built in 1894 for a school roll of 798 children. It was formerly known as **Stuart Secondary School** and stood on the long-vanished Sussex Road, which was obliterated in the 1970s to build the Moorlands Estate that surrounds the school. It included a domestic science and a manual trades instruction centre. The locally listed building is an imposing three- and four-storey edifice of stock brick with red brick detailing, and a plain clay tile roof with dormers and tall chimneys.

Richard Atkins Primary School on **New Park Road** was built in 1897 (architect T.J. Bailey - bottom right

photo) and extended in 1903 - it is Grade II listed. It has a classic LSB layout of stair towers at each end, surmounted by ogee cupolas with lower linking sections to the end blocks which have shaped gables embellished by finials and bulls eye windows. The southern wing has a stone plaque with the original name - **Brixton Hill School**.

The former **Charles Edward Brooke** School on **Cormont Road** has a majestic frontage overlooking Myatt's Fields Park. Designed by Bailey for 894 pupils and opened in 1898, it was extended by the LCC in 1912. Its large symmetrical façade has a central section of three storeys flanked by six-storey towers with spires crowned with octagonal turrets. The high pitched roof has three small lucernes (dormers). The Historic England (Grade II) listing entry righty describes it as 'a building of romance and fantasy'. It was requisitioned as a hospital in the First World War and was later known as Cormont Secondary School. Top photos: 2016 and 1916.

The former **Kennington Road School**, later known as Vauxhall Manor School Annexe (now flats, named **The Lycee**) is a late example of the palatial Victorian triple-decker design dating from 1897 for 894 pupils (architect T.J. Bailey - middle photo). It has a central five-bay block under a hipped roof with tiny dormers and flanking six-storey staircase towers with ogee pyramidal roofs. It is pictured in c1920 in the bottom photo with a London County Council tram passing down Kennington Road. It is Grade II listed.

The last three board schools built at the end of the century are a prelude to a different approach to school design that was to follow in the 1900s. They are all of a smaller, more domestic scale than the grand triple-deckers, having one and two storeys. **Henry Cavendish School** on **Hydethorpe Road** in Balham by Bailey (top view) was built in 1898. **Rosendale Road Junior School** on **Turney Road** in West Dulwich (listed Grade II, middle photo) was designed by Bailey, with a roll of 750 pupils. It was opened in 1900 and extended in 1905. The centre block has paired central gables divided by a chimney with a slender cupola behind.

Sunnyhill Primary School in Streatham is by Robson and opened in 1901 (bottom photos). It is listed Grade II. The two-bay front on Valley Road has a pair of pedimented gables and dramatic paired chimneys with one-storey side and rear ranges. The west wing has an unusual tall narrow copper fleche (spire) seen in the photo below taken in 1971 with the long-demolished half-timbered United Dairies (later Unigate) building on Valley Road in the background.

PARKS

Lambeth is a borough blessed with over 60 parks and open spaces; many of them dating back to the Victorian era when great importance was attached to laying out green spaces for the enjoyment, recreation and health of city dwellers. The much older commons of Clapham, Tooting and Streatham changed little in this period except for additions such as the elegant cast-iron bandstand on Clapham Common originally erected in Kensington in 1861 and moved here by the London County Council in 1890, and cafe pavilions on all three commons.

Kennington Park was the exception - Kennington Common was a marshy area in the 17th century used for grazing, for recreation and for the public execution of criminals including murderers, traitors and highwaymen. By the 18th century it hosted games of cricket, quoits and bowls as well as gatherings for prayer and protest, the executions also continuing. The top left engraving dates from 1842. In 1848 it hosted a mass protest meeting by the Chartists, a movement for political reform. In 1852 the common was enclosed, iron boundary railings erected and landscaping laid out to create a formal park (middle photo: c1910). It was acquired by the LCC from the Duchy of Cornwall in 1889 and the pretty refreshment house (below), which still serves the park today, was erected in 1897. The park is registered Grade II.

Myatt's Fields Park in West Camberwell is a well preserved example of a late-Victorian park. The site was a market garden for much of the 19th century until it was donated by the local landowner, William Minet to the Metropolitan Public Gardens Association, which laid out the park. It opened in 1889. It was designed by one of the very few female landscape gardeners of the time, Fanny Wilkinson, who planned gravelled serpentine paths, greenhouses, shrubberies, lawns and flower beds. A wealth of original features remain such as the bandstand (top left photo), the circular pavilion (top right) and the park keeper's lodge seen in the top middle view of 1890 (though sadly not the adjacent lych-gate) The park is registered Grade II.

Vauxhall Park, seen in the middle photo and the bottom layout plan of 1888, was opened by the Prince of Wales (later King Edward VII) in 1890, following a campaign by the Kyrle Society and their treasurer Octavia Hill. It was also designed by Fanny Wilkinson, but few original features remain (see the Fawcett statue entry on page 207).

Brockwell Park (Grade II registered on the National Heritage List) is one of the finest parks in London, extending over 50 hectares with views from its summit across the capital. It was laid out by the LCC and opened by Lord Rosebery in 1892 following a campaign led by Thomas Bristowe, MP for Norwood (whose bust is displayed in Brockwell Hall, the 1820s mansion preserved at the heart of the park). A number of historic structures in the park survive including the beautiful walled garden, stable block, lodge on Norwood Road and the clock tower (1897), but sadly not the bandstand pictured here in 1905. The lido was added in 1937.

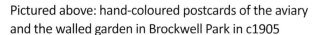

Pictured above: hand-coloured postcards of the aviary and the walled garden in Brockwell Park in c1905

Archbishop's Park once formed part of the grounds of Lambeth Palace, home of Archbishops of Canterbury since the 13th century. The eastern half of the grounds of the palace comprising nine acres, were first used for public recreation in the 1890s. This was formalised in 1900 when the Church Commissioners granted a licence for it to become a public park and it was divided from the remainder of the palace gardens by a high new wall.

The park was laid out by the LCC and it opened in 1901. The lawns, children's playground and games courts have served the north of the borough ever since. The oldest structure in the park, the timber framed, tiled roofed shelter (pictured below left) was recently restored. In the south western corner of the park was a lake (pictured below right in c1905 with the Palace in the background) but this was filled in by the 1930s. The Millennium Pathway in the centre of the park highlights moments in the borough's history up to the year 2000.

SHOPS

By the end of the 19th century Brixton, Clapham, Streatham and West and Upper Norwood were all important and thriving shopping centres characterised by parades of shops offering a wide variety of goods and services. Most of these were small independent traders who often lived above their shops, though by the end of the century multiple stores were becoming established. One such example is **David Greig** who opened his first store at **54-58 Atlantic Road** in Brixton in 1870. Now a bar it still retains most of its ochre and oxblood tiled shopfront - see top right photo below. The bottom right view below shows another of the retailer's shopfronts at **232 Coldharbour Lane** opened in c1890, a third shopfront and interior survives at **177 Streatham High Road** (Grade II listed, c1900). This period also heralded the golden age of the department store - large emporiums selling a wide range of products under one roof, such as Pratts in Streatham, and in Brixton, the Bon Marché, Morley & Lanceley (founded in 1880 and still trading today as Morleys), Francis & Son at 448-450 Brixton Road (see their advert from 1889, below) which is now Marks & Spencer's, and Quin & Axten.

Street markets flourished in Brixton and on streets between Vauxhall and The Cut including Lambeth Walk and Lower Marsh. As the population grew, older houses had single-storey 'bungalow' shop premises built over their front gardens up to the pavement as can still be seen today, notably on Clapham High Street and Kennington Road.

Perhaps the most famous street in Brixton is **Electric Avenue**, laid out in 1888 and said to be the first shopping street in London to be lit by electricity, hence its name. The illustration below shows the street from Brixton Road soon after completion, the elegant curve toward Atlantic Road evident in the background. Cast iron and glass canopies were soon added on each side of the street (seen in the bottom right photo of c1920) though these had become near-derelict by the end of the 1970s and were removed. The avenue is a set-piece of late-Victorian town planning - the gracious four-storey parades of shops with flats above are of stock brick with red brick pilasters and pedimented stone window architraves, timber dormers within slate mansards, tall chimney stacks, and two surviving cupolas, one at each end. The entire composition is locally listed.

The avenue suffered a direct hit in the Second World War on the south west corner of its junction with Electric Lane, replaced in the 1950s by flat roofed two-storey shops. Only the left-hand gateway block, seen in the 1888 image (left) survives, the right-hand one having been redeveloped in the 1930s (the Boots store).

The top image is a very atmospheric photo taken in 1964 of Brixton's Victorian heritage looking north up Electric Lane from Electric Avenue towards the railway viaduct (1861) and the Railway Hotel (1880 - see entry on page 93). Note the glazed canopy in this view.

A fine and rare Victorian Gothic shopfront at **310-312 Brixton Road** built in 1879 survives thanks to its Grade II listing in 1981 (bottom left view). It has beautiful red sandstone piers with gabled tops and a pair of painted timber shopfronts with wrought iron stallriser and door grills.

A purpose-built butcher's premises with living accommodation over, built as part of a shopping parade in 1891, survives remarkably intact at **296 Brixton Hill** (photo bottom right). It later became a dental laboratory but its shopfront and interior were little altered and it was listed Grade II in 2002. Inside, the shop is lined in brown and white veined marble with a varnished timber cashiers' counter at the rear.

Brixton town centre's flagship was the **Bon Marché Department Store, 442-444 Brixton Road**, said to be the first purpose-built department store in England. It opened in 1877 and was designed by Lambeth architects, Messrs H. Parsons & Rawlings, modelled on the Parisian department store, offering a wide variety of goods under one roof. It became part of the Selfridge group in 1926 and then John Lewis in 1940, finally closing in 1975. The locally listed building is now occupied by shops and offices. Top and bottom right photos: 1910, photo to left: c1965.

Parades and individual shops were built across the borough, some examples are illustrated here.

The top and middle right photos (the latter taken in c1910) are of **401** (locally listed) and **403-405 Brixton Road**, both good examples of later Victorian high street architecture, the former in a French Gothic style, the latter in the banded Queen Anne idiom. The bottom left photo is of **Llewelyns, 293-295 Railton Road** in Herne Hill, which has a particularly good late Victorian shopfront of curved glass (see also photo of c1920 on page 68).

The view below is of the Grade II listed mid-Victorian **2-26 Queenstown Road**, a magnificent Gothic-style parade with gabled dormers by J.T. Knowles (1864).

Photos clockwise from top left: **827-837 Wandsworth Road** by J.T. Knowles (1865) - a three-storey terrace of grey brick with stucco window architraves decorated with vine leaves; an unbroken, graceful, sweeping parade of 20 shops at **463-501 Norwood Road** in West Norwood (1894) which are of red brick with pointed gables and highly decorated spandrel panels between the first- and second-floor windows; the stately corner-towered **Dover House, 170 Westminster Bridge Road** by Treadwell & Martin (1897) built in the Jacobean revival style, now the Co-op, and the charming **Abbeville Road** in Clapham (55-71 pictured here built by W. Peacock in 1892).

Another popular shopping district soon developed along the length of **Streatham High Road**, boosted by the opening of Pratt's Department Store in the 1850s, which served Streatham until its closure in 1990 (see page 190). Elegant parades of shops were built in the 1870s-90s, two of the finest examples are **207-211** (top engraving of 1885, little changed today except for new shopfronts) and **324-342** (1885), both by Frederick Wheeler. The latter parade is seen on the left of the middle photo of c1900 with all its shop blinds extended and in the present-day bottom left view - note the dramatic roofline of Dutch gables, the curved fish-scale tiled roof on the former bank premises at 324, and the elevations of red brick with horizontal stone banding.

The **Beehive Coffee Tavern, 496 Streatham High Road** (photo below) was designed by Ernest George and built in 1878 by the temperance movement. Sited next to the Pied Bull pub, it was intended to provide an alternative non-alcoholic attraction for the workers of the adjacent rubber factory. The Grade II listed building is of brick with casement window dormers which have pargetted gables, the hall behind having a steeply pitched tiled roof and taller dormers. It is now offices.

BANKS

A series of mergers between smaller banks and the creation of large nationwide banks in the later Victorian period resulted in the construction of imposing new bank premises throughout Britain. Grand banking halls with polished oak counters and bronze screens were often a feature, as was a flat for the manager on one of the upper floors. All architectural styles were utilised including Gothic, classical, 'Tudorbethan', baroque and neo-Georgian. Lambeth has some very fine examples, though sadly this building type is greatly under-represented on the National Heritage List and none in the borough are listed, although some have been locally listed in recent years.

Pictured here is the well preserved **Barclays** branch, **188 Clapham High Street** on the corner of Venn Street. It was built in 1895 by the London & South Western Bank (L&SW) which was acquired by Barclays in 1918. The top photo was taken in c1905 with a tram and an omnibus in the foreground, both horse-drawn. It has a grand corner bay topped by a cupola and weathervane; the four-storey façades are of a warm red brick with elaborate cream-painted stone dressings. The original tall chimney stacks, slate roofs with clay decorative ridge tiles and dormers surmounted by broken circular semi-pediments set within grandiose gables, crown this magnificent locally listed landmark.

Upper Norwood has two good examples of Victorian bank architecture. The former **Barclays Bank** at **61 Westow Hill** was built in by the L&SW Bank in 1871 (top photo: 1963), closing in 2015. It has stucco elevations, the rusticated ground floor is embellished with stone masks representing the different continents, and there is a semi-circular balustrade over the corner entrance. The former **London & County Bank** at **77a Westow Hill**, in later years a branch of the National Westminster and now an estate agents, was designed by Horace Chesterton and built in 1884 (see images bottom left and below). It has richly decorated façades of red brick with swag motifs below the cornice, a rusticated stucco

ground floor, fluted pilasters and a commanding triangular pediment on the canted corner facing towards the site of the Crystal Palace (burnt down in 1936).

The locally listed **NatWest Bank** at **89-95 Westminster Bridge Road** (bottom right view) is a dignified composition of 1894 in red brick with rusticated piers and ball finials above the parapet.

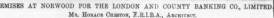

PREMISES AT NORWOOD FOR THE LONDON AND COUNTY BANKING CO., LIMITED. Mr. Horace Cheston, F.R.I.B.A., Architect.

The **former Barclays Bank** at **139-141 Streatham High Road** was built in 1893 by the L&SW Bank. It has a rendered ground floor with pink granite composite columns and arched windows to the banking hall (top right photo: 1960). Bottom photos: c1933 and 1951.

136-140 Herne Hill was built by the **London & Westminster Bank** in 1898 (top photo: 1910, bottom left: 2016). It became a NatWest branch after a merger in 1968, closing in 1993. It was then converted into an Indian restaurant and since 2010 it has been a Pizza Express. It has mellow yellow stock brick elevations, the dressings and the ground floor façades being of contrasting red brick and terracotta. Shaped gables and tall chimneys punctuate the roofline. It was designed by Frederick William Hunt, who also designed the Grade II* listed St Luke's Church of 1883-92 on the border of Clapham and Balham in Wandsworth.

Another former **National Westminster Bank** stands at **27 Norwood Road** (locally listed, photo above right). It was built by the London & County Bank (whose emblem within a stone tablet still graces the side elevation) at the end of the Victorian era in 1901. It was designed by Bartleet & Sons - W.G. Bartleet also designed the Grade II* listed Church of St George, Beckenham of 1885-1903. It has proud classical Italianate elevations of red brick and Portland stone dressings above a rusticated Portland stone ground floor. The bank branch closed in 2012 and it is now an estate agents.

TRANSPORT

Westminster Bridge is one of the most elegant of the Thames crossings which perfectly complements the dramatic backdrop of the Houses of Parliament (built 1840-1870). Its seven graceful semi-elliptical spans spring from piers faced with grey Cornish granite above the elegant cutwaters. Its cast iron balustrade is in the Gothic style with quatrefoils and it has Tudor-Gothic cast-iron lamp standards. The Grade II* listed bridge was designed by the civil engineer Thomas Page and architect of the Palace of Westminster, Charles Barry. It opened in 1862, replacing an earlier bridge of 1750 which had suffered from subsidence. Bottom photos: c1880 & c1905.

Vauxhall railway station was opened in 1848 when the London & South Western Railway extended its mainline into Waterloo, replacing its original terminus at Nine Elms, where the New Covent Garden Flower Market is now. The single-storey station entrance block is a handsome classical design (top photo). The locally listed building has five arched openings with ashlar pilasters and keystones, the roof concealed behind the cornice and parapet. The middle view of 1910 shows the station and its bustling forecourt with the tall walls above the viaduct screening the eight elevated platforms.

Streatham Hill station is pictured below (right hand view: 1919). It was opened by the London, Brighton & South Coast Railway (LBSCR) in 1856. The single-storey ticket hall straddles the tracks and platforms in the cutting below. It has attractive weatherboard elevations and a hipped slated roof. It is an increasingly rare example of early railway architecture, which was often modest and of a simple timber construction. Sadly it was rejected for listing by English Heritage.

Gipsy Hill station (top photo) was also opened on the same line in 1856, but the current ticket office, perched on the overbridge above the tracks, was rebuilt in red brick later in the Victorian era. It is pictured middle left In c1912 and apart from a minor modification to the left hand window opening to form a new accessible entrance, has changed little, retaining its LBSCR coat of arms on each gable end and glazed entrance canopy with decorative timber valance. The attractive weatherboard building and canopy on platform one also survives.

Clapham High Street station (bottom photo), was opened by the London, Chatham & Dover Railway (LCDR) in 1862, when it was named simply Clapham station. It was given its present name in 1989 to avoid confusion with Clapham Junction. In 1909 it was served by the first electrified suburban service in London, running from Victoria to London Bridge. It is now served by the London Overground.

The station originally had two platforms, enlarged to four in 1867 but reduced again to the original two in 1916. The original Gothic-style station building on Voltaire Road survives and is Grade II listed though it ceased to be in railway use in the 1970s and was used as a clothing workshop/furniture emporium until its conversion to flats in 2006. It is of stock brick with a cill course and flush bands of pale and red terracotta. The openings have flattened Gothic arches and below the overhanging eaves of the hipped-slated roofs run richly decorated cornices of projecting brickwork.

Herne Hill station was also opened in 1862 by the LCDR in what was then, and is still today, a well-to-do area of villas for the professional classes. The Grade II listed building has a lofty tower with blind arcading and a pyramidal roof. This is attached to a two-storey six bay block of stock brick with bands of white brick and red dressings to the Gothic windows. The wooden valanced forecourt canopy was restored in 2016. The top photo dates from c1920 and the bottom left photo of c1900 shows the original layout before the present twin island platforms were built in 1925 as part of the electrification of the line to Orpington by the Southern Railway.

Tulse Hill station (bottom right photo) was opened in 1868 by the LBSCR on their line into London Bridge, becoming an important junction station the following year when the line from Blackfriars (now Thameslink) was extended to Wimbledon in 1871. The original station building of stock brick with red brick dressings survives little altered, though the original trainshed over all four platforms was replaced by individual canopies in the 1900s. The island platform canopy was replaced by a utilitarian canopy in the 1960s.

The **Hungerford Railway Bridge** (top photo) replaced Isambard Kingdom Brunel's suspension footbridge of 1845 (see Lost Lambeth on p.182) but reused Brunel's red brick piers. Serving the Charing Cross terminus, the bridge opened in 1864. It comprises nine spans of wrought iron lattice girders and was designed by Sir John Hawkshaw (middle photo: c1864). The Golden Jubilee footbridges were added either side in 2002.

The **railway bridges** over **Rosendale Road** (bottom left view) and over **Croxted Road** (the western half of which lies in Lambeth, the eastern in Southwark) were designed by Charles Barry Junior in his role as surveyor to the Dulwich Estate and built in 1866. The former is of a yellow and red brick with an elliptical arch over the roadway and two round arches over the footways, framed by rusticated pilasters. It is Grade II listed. The locally listed bridge at the northern end of **Croxted Road** (photo below) has a modern bridge deck but retains its very fine cast iron framework and rusticated brick abutments. A second bridge across this road to the south was rebuilt in 2014, leaving only the grand abutments bearing the restored decorative crests of the LBSCR and the landowner, Dulwich College.

The **Knight's Hill tunnel** built in 1866-68 was designed by Robert Jacomb-Hood (1822-1900) who was the LBSCR's chief engineer and surveyor from 1846 until 1860 when he set up his own practice but continued to work on the railway company's projects until his death. The imposing locally listed tunnel portals either side of the 302 metre long tunnel comprise polychromatic red and yellow brickwork, a dentil cornice and the railway company's coat of arms on the cartouche at the centre of the parapet.

The Grade II listed frontage block to the former **London Necropolis Railway Terminus** at **121 Westminster Bridge Road** (bottom photo) is a monumental late-Victorian edifice built in 1900-02. It has a granite arched entrance, upper floors of rusticated brickwork and a terracotta columned centrepiece surmounted by a pair of pediments decorated with a cartouche and fronds of Art Nouveau ornament. It replaced the original terminus to the west which had opened in 1854. Trains conveyed coffins and funeral corteges to Brookwood Cemetery in Surrey. The station behind was destroyed by a bomb in 1941 and the service was discontinued.

On the facing page are six images of the Victorian railway infrastructure that dominates Brixton's townscape. The top left and middle left views are of the two bridges that stride over **Brixton Road** (photos taken in 1948 and 2016). The top right view is of a steam train entering Brixton station (opened in 1862) in c1930, note the Bon Marché department store in the background. The middle right photo is of **Atlantic Road** in c1910. The bottom left photo taken in c1940 is of a steam train on the viaduct high above **Brixton Station Road** with fine semaphore signals and the signal box straddling the tracks in the background. The bottom right view taken in c1910 is of the **Marks & Spencer's Penny Bazaar**, which occupied a railway arch on Station Road before moving to their present-day store at 446 Brixton Road in 1931.

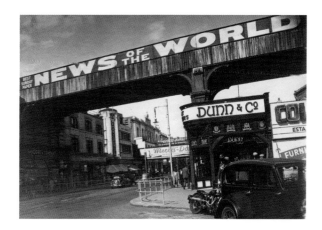

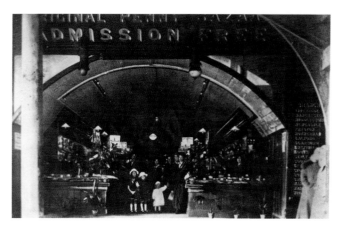

INDUSTRY

Manufacturing industry has been a rarity in Lambeth since the 1960s but in the 19th century it was found in most districts of the borough, often cheek-by-jowl with housing. Featured here are surviving examples of industrial buildings across Lambeth, most of which are now in office or residential use.

The top and bottom left (c1920) photographs are of the former **Eagle Printing Works** of 1864 (as proudly inscribed at cornice level) at **304-306 Brixton Road**. Its muscular well embellished brickwork façade survives remarkably little altered.

The **former Plough Brewery** at **156 Wandsworth Road** (bottom right photo) was home to the brewers Thomas Woodward & Son from 1869 to 1925 and then Simonds but has been business units since 1968. The Grade II listed building is of yellow brick with a low pitched slate roof. Its double-height central carriage arch has rusticated stone jambs and voussoirs.

Doulton's ceramics are known the world over - the **Doulton** family established a new works on Lambeth High Street in 1846 and by the 1860s were specialising in industrial ceramics such as drainage pipes and sanitary fittings, and also in domestic and ornamental salt-glazed stoneware such

as that used for ornate fireplace surrounds (an Edwardian example is pictured below). In the 1870s they built palatial new buildings on **Black Prince Road** (now offices named **Southbank House** pictured top and in the bottom left engraving of 1876) and south of Salamanca Street on the Albert Embankment. The latter were vacated in 1940 and tragically demolished in the mid-1950s when Victorian architecture was widely despised - see page 200 in the Lost Lambeth chapter. The surviving Southbank House has beautiful Grade II listed façades of pink and beige terracotta decorated with plant and owl motifs with a tympanum relief by Doulton's in-house sculptor George Tinworth of craftsmen examining vases.

Another important industrial landmark in the borough is Sir Joseph **Causton and Sons** former printing works at **139-143 Clapham Road**. The T-shaped building has a long 17-bay four-storey frontage of stock brick with red brick quoins and window headers (top photos). The locally listed building was designed at the end of Victoria's reign and was occupied by Freeman's mail order company from 1937, which added vast extensions in the 1930-50s. The building was damaged during World War II with a direct hit on a shelter, killing 23 employees. Freemans left the site in c2004 and the frontage building was converted to 35 flats with a further 152 flats and 18 houses built on the rest of the site. Top right photo: c1914.

The photo below left is of **Vintage House** - the last remaining industrial building on the **Albert Embankment (36-37)** - the four-storey stock brick façade of six bays has red brick segmental arches over the windows. It is now offices. **379a Kennington Road** (bottom right) is a tall and slender four-storey mid-Victorian warehouse which would look equally at home on a typical Main Street in a North American town.

245 Coldharbour Lane (and 100-104 Shakespeare Road) was built in 1887 as a corn merchants' premises; it was later known as the **Coldharbour Works** (top photo: 1965, middle photo: 2016). The locally listed building comprises a three-storey warehouse with two gables and loading bays on the upper floors, offices, and a shop. It is built of stock brick with red brick and stone dressings.

The **former Hollis & Son furniture polish factory** at **10-11 Bishops Terrace** in Kennington is another notable survival of Lambeth's now scarce industrial heritage (bottom left view). Built in 1898 it is a well preserved three-storey building of stock brick with red brick and blue engineering brick dressings with small paned metal framed windows. The central bay has loading bay doors and an iron gantry used to lift goods up to the upper floors. A stable block is attached. Both are Grade II listed.

Pictured below is the former **New London Brewery** on **Durham Street**, Vauxhall, built in c1889, which later became part of the Marmite yeast extract factory (1927-67) and is now the **Westminster Business Centre**. Behind the very well detailed two-storey yellow brick gabled office building is a five-storey structure with an oriel window.

The Oval Gasworks was originally the South London Waterworks which had two brick-lined circular reservoirs and an engine house built in 1807. The company left the site in 1845 and sold it to the **Phoenix Gas Light & Coke Company**. They adapted the circular reservoirs for gasholder tanks and erected five gasometers between 1847 and 1874. One was converted to a spiral-guided holder in 1950 (which does not require a frame) and another was removed in 1975. Of the four that remain, only one, Gasholder 1 (built in 1892 to replace the smaller original No. 1 gasometer) is Grade II listed by virtue of it being the world's largest gasholder at the time, its noted designers - Frank and George Livesey, and also because it is an internationally renowned backdrop to matches at the adjacent Oval Cricket Ground. The adjoining Gasholders 4 & 5 erected in 1874 and 1876 (top left photo), were designed by Sir Corbet Woodall and are locally listed. They have elegant neo-classical style frames and Tuscan columns. The gasometers were decommissioned in 2014 and the site is due for redevelopment, sadly it is likely that only the nationally listed No. 1 gasometer will be preserved. The middle view shows a game in progress in c1860 with one of the gasometers in the background. The bottom left view is of the Grade II listed No.1 gasholder from Montford Place in 1965. The aerial photo below was taken in 1934.

PUBLIC HOUSES

Only a selection of Victorian pubs in Lambeth can be covered here - to include all would require its own book. A Lambeth Planning study in 2013 recorded 179 pubs operating and a further 118 that had closed since the 1950s, many having ceased trading since 2000. The vast majority of these 297 pubs in the borough were either established during the Victorian period or were older hostelries that were rebuilt during this period. This chapter features 70 examples and includes most of those that are nationally or locally listed.

Pubs of North Lambeth

The former **Mason's Arms, 17 Lambeth Road** was rebuilt in c1890 and renamed the **Lambeth Walk** in 1951 (top left and bottom left photos: 1965 & 2016). It closed in 2010 and was converted into flats. It is a solid rectangular stock brick building with red brick segmental arches and stuccoed keystones to the sash windows and a robust bracketed cornice. The famous jazz pianist Sir George Shearing began his career here in the 1930s before emigrating to find international fame in the USA.

The former **Angel, 73 Lambeth Walk** is now a tourist hostel (bottom right). It was rebuilt in c1890 with a cheerful façade of banded red and stock brick pilasters with pedimented tripartite windows to the first floor and paired windows on the second beneath giant red brick arches.

The Pineapple, 53 Hercules Road (top left) was built in 1870 and is exceptionally fine. It has a well-detailed pub front with red granite columns and elaborate capitals in the Gothic Revival style. The stock brick upper floors are richly decorated with stucco architraves, spandrels and cornice. It is locally listed.

Two locally listed pubs grace **Lower Marsh**, an ancient street lined with market stalls. **The Spanish Patriot** at **34** (now **Lounge 34** - bottom left) was rebuilt in 1890 by J.W. Brooker, architect of the Grade II* listed Half Moon in Herne Hill. The façades have red and white bands of brickwork at first-floor level with grey brick above articulated by rubbed red brick pilasters with a palm tree motif, crowned by a gable and a corner pediment.

The Camel & Artichoke at **121** (top right, formerly **The Artichoke**) was rebuilt in 1878 by H.J. Newton. It has a distinguished elevation of grey brickwork, arcaded at first-floor level and a traditional pub frontage with a haulingway through to the back yard.

The westernmost half of **The Wellington, 81 Waterloo Road** (top left) was originally a separate hostelry called the **Lord Hill**. It was built in 1891. Its locally listed striped red brick and sandstone façade is crowned by a tall shaped gable and an octagonal cupola.

The Stage Door (formerly the **Halfway House**) **28-30 Webber Street** (bottom left) was rebuilt in c1890. Above the traditional pub front with its composite columns is an attractive façade of red brick with rubbed brick spandrel panels. It is locally listed.

The King's Arms, 25 Roupell Street (bottom right photo) dates from c1840. It has simple stock brick elevations with stucco window surrounds and a pub frontage enlivened by fluted pilasters with floral capitals. It is Grade II listed.

Pubs of Kennington

The Duchy Arms (the **Anchor & Hope** until 1972), **63 Sancroft Street** (top photo) is a fine mid-19th century corner pub in the heart of the Duchy of Cornwall's Kennington Estate - three simple Italianate street elevations, arched pub windows, and quoins to the first floor.

The locally listed **White Hart** (now the **Tommyfield** - bottom left photo), **185 Kennington Lane**, was opened in c1746 and rebuilt in 1897. Its warm red brick and terracotta façade is an impressive landmark on Kennington Cross.

The Grade II listed **Hanover Arms, 326 Kennington Park Road** (below right) dates from c1840 and has plain early Victorian-style upper elevations of stock brick with a stucco trim, the rounded corner turning into Hanover Gardens. The projecting pub front dates from c1910.

The Roebuck (now the **Dog House**), **293 Kennington Road** was rebuilt in 1877. The prow ended façades facing Kennington Cross have timber pub frontages with beautiful red granite pilasters and stallrisers. The arcaded first floor has stucco arches framing the sash windows. The pub is locally listed.

Below this recent view is another photo taken in c1922 of this whole stretch of Kennington Road showing the Roebuck on the right, the Georgian terraces built in c1790 to the north and the spire of St Philip's Church in the background behind the electric tram (see entry in Lost Lambeth chapter on page 173).

The Ship, 171 Kennington Road (top photo) was rebuilt in c1840 on the site of an end of terrace mid-Georgian pub of c1780. It has simple upper elevations with elegant stucco cornice, sash windows and a curved 'hinge' on the corner above an attractive pub front - the fascia supported on polished granite pilasters. **The Grand Union** (formerly the **Tankard**), **111 Kennington Road** stands on the corner of Brook Drive. The middle left view shows it today, with its grandiose façade as rebuilt in 1879, making an interesting comparison with the middle right view of its predecessor in c1875 - a much simpler rendered design.

The Three Stags, 67-69 Kennington Road, (bottom photo) is another Georgian pub rebuilt by the Victorians on what was then, and is still today, one of Lambeth's finest and most gracious thoroughfares. It faces the important crossroads where Lambeth Road and Kennington Road meet. The architect was Alfred Wright and it was completed in 1891. The upper storeys are of stock brick with imposing tripartite sash windows. The refined pub frontage retains its original pilasters and Art Nouveau detailing to the capitals, leaded pane top-lights, scrolled pediments and the intricate ironwork balustrade above the dentil cornice. All three pubs are locally listed.

The Golden Goose (formerly **The Union Tavern**), **146 Camberwell New Road**, top left) has a striking façade with a two-storey curving cast iron veranda, gables and a tower with a belvedere and a weathervane. It was rebuilt in c1890.

The Kennington (formerly **The Skinner's Arms**), **60 Camberwell New Road** (bottom left) built in c1900, has handsome elevations of striped red brick and stone with decorated gables and a copper dome on the corner of Foxley Road.

The Fentiman Arms, 64 Fentiman Road, (below) is a popular and well-preserved early-Victorian corner pub of c1850. The upper-floor façade is of stock brick with pedimented windows to the first floor. The fine pub front has pilasters, a modillion cornice and arched openings which have decorative spandrels. All three pubs are locally listed.

Pubs of Vauxhall

The Royal Vauxhall Tavern, 372 Kennington Lane was built in 1862, probably by the architect James Edmeston the Elder, as part of his scheme to redevelop the Vauxhall Pleasure Gardens that had closed in 1859. It has a quadrant footprint and a curved façade of stock brick with stucco dressings and four arched bays terminating at each end by pedimented bookends. It was listed Grade II in 2015 by virtue of its architectural interest and its cultural history since the 1950s as one of London's longest established gay pubs. Top and bottom left photos: 1950 and 2016.

The locally listed former **Elephant & Castle, 2 South Lambeth Place** (photos top and bottom right: c1970 and 2016) was rebuilt in the c1870s and is now a Starbucks cafe. It has ornate upper-floor sash window surrounds, c1910s tiled pub frontage, and a superb pair of elephant and castle sculptures at parapet level on both elevations.

The Vauxhall Griffin (formerly the **Builders Arms**), **8 Wyvil Road**, (top left) has simple brick elevations and sash windows, four blind recesses, one sporting a griffin sign board, and a well-preserved pub front which has plain pilasters, cornice and fascia. It was built in c1870 when it was a simple corner pub in an area of terraced houses, light industry and the Nine Elms railway goods depot, all long gone and even their 20th century successors such as the Keybridge House British Telecom building of 1976 replaced by high rise housing to the north and west.

The former **Wheatsheaf** (now **Tia Maria** restaurant), **126 South Lambeth Road** (c1870 - photo top right) has a fine façade - an arcaded first floor, original Jacobean-style pub front with a cartouche and a dramatic brick and stucco chimney stack.

The Royal Oak, 355 Kennington Lane (bottom left), was rebuilt on a grand scale in 1891. It has an outstanding pub front which retains its original joinery and etched and leaded glass. All three pubs are locally listed.

The Jolly Gardeners, 49-51 Black Prince Road (top photo) has a traditional pub front, red brick and stucco striped frontages, and a decorative plaque depicting two gardeners. Rebuilt by architects Lewcock and Grierson in 1895, it is now a German gastropub named **Zeitgeist**.

The Queen's Head, 71 Black Prince Road (now a café - bottom left) has Flemish-style shaped gables. It was rebuilt in 1890. Charlie Chaplain's uncle was the publican here in 1900. It is also pictured below in 1965 when it was owned by Courage's Brewery - the elevations remarkably little changed to this day. Both pubs are locally listed.

The Black Dog, 112 Vauxhall Walk was rebuilt in 1895 (top) and is a well-restored local pub with fine Queen Anne-style red brick façades, elaborate gables and a pub front with tiled stallrisers.

The Rose (formerly **The Crown**), **35 Albert Embankment** (bottom left) was built in c1880. It has Venetian Revival-style elevations with arched windows and a fine curved-glass window and crown motif on the corner.

The Tea House Theatre (the former **Queen Anne** - photo bottom right), **139 Vauxhall Walk** has a fine gabled brick façade and timber pub front. It has a rich history since it opened in 1886, from being a local pub serving a tight-knit working class neighbourhood of terraced housing and manufacturing industry (cleared in the 1970s to create the Vauxhall Pleasure gardens park), to a striptease bar from the 1950s until 2010. It is now a very pleasant cafe and a music and theatre venue. All three pubs are locally listed.

Pubs of Brixton

The White Horse, 94 Brixton Hill is a three-storey pub (top photo) on the site of an 18th century coaching inn. It was rebuilt in c1875 and is seen in the bottom left image in c1905 with a tram passing in front of it. It has an asymmetrical three-storey façade with a pediment over the carriage arch on the right hand side leading to a rear yard and semi-circular headed sash windows to the first floor. It is locally listed.

The Telegraph, 228 Brixton Hill (bottom right view) was designed by W.M. Bruton and built in 1896. It has an ornate exterior topped with a grand shaped central gable and flattened domes on the bays to either side with tiered finials. The pub closed in 2009.

The Elm Park Tavern, 76 Elm Park in Brixton Hill (photo above) dates from c1875 and has pleasing upper façades of stock brick and red brick dressings matching its residential neighbours built at the same time. It has a shallow pitched hipped slate roof with dormers. Its simple pub frontage has fluted pilasters of stucco and retains its fine historic joinery and stained glass. It is locally listed.

The former **George IV, 144 Brixton Hill** is now a Tesco Express (pictured above). It is a good example of late-Victorian pub architecture - a great contrast from the much simpler designs of the first half of the queen's reign. The local list entry describes its *"exuberant freestyle... Moorish arch and other fancy detailing to the pilasters and consoles ... pink granite stallriser and oriel corner bay rising to the conical copper dome"*. It was erected in c1895.

The former **George Canning** (now the **Hootananny**) at **95 Effra Road** is pictured here in 2016 and c1905. It was rebuilt in 1896 on the site of its 1820s predecessor. It has an Italianate arcaded loggia at first floor with a swept copper roof, two long pub frontages of fine joinery and a copper dome on the Brixton Water Lane elevation.

The **Effra Hall Tavern, 38 Kellet Road** (top left photo on the facing page) has occupied this commanding corner site since 1876 with a fine arcaded first floor and original pub front.

The Landor (formerly the Landor Hotel) at **70 Landor Road** was built in 1881 (top right and bottom photos on the facing page) and has elevations of stock brick with stucco dressings. The interior has a superb mirrored bar with a theatre on the first floor. All three pubs are locally listed.

Three Brixton town centre pubs of great character are pictured here. They reflect the changes in the architectural styles of the Victorian era. **The Trinity Arms, 45 Trinity Square** (1850 - top photo) with its low mansard roof is of a simple classical design. The ground-floor faience frontage was remodelled in the interwar years. It is locally listed.

The former **Atlantic** (now the **Dogstar**), **389 Coldharbour Lane** (bottom left) is a classic corner pub of 1868 with bays of stock brick framing a stuccoed prow, classical balustrade, window surrounds and pediments.

The 1860s former **Black Horse, 393 Brixton Road** (bottom right) is now a branch of the Halifax bank but still retains its elegant upper storeys of arched windows and rusticated quoins. The canted corner bay has an ornate pediment inscribed with the name of the pub, topped by obelisks.

The **Railway Tavern**, (now the **Wahaca** Mexican restaurant) **20 Atlantic Road**, was designed by R. Cruwys and built in 1880 (top). It has a flat-iron footprint. The hexagonal clock tower with its spire and six clock faces is one of Brixton's most important landmarks standing with railway viaducts on all three sides. The former **Green Man, 225 Coldharbour Lane** (middle right) has stood at the heart of Loughborough Junction since c1865. It has been well restored as a training centre. **The Loughborough Hotel, 39 Loughborough Road** was built in 1900 (bottom photos: 2016 and c1905) and included a fine ballroom. This imposing landmark of red brick and stucco is now flats above a gallery in the former pub. All three public houses are locally listed.

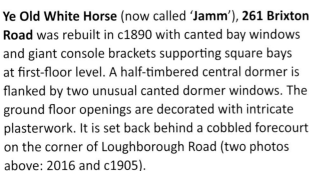

Ye Old White Horse (now called '**Jamm**'), **261 Brixton Road** was rebuilt in c1890 with canted bay windows and giant console brackets supporting square bays at first-floor level. A half-timbered central dormer is flanked by two unusual canted dormer windows. The ground floor openings are decorated with intricate plasterwork. It is set back behind a cobbled forecourt on the corner of Loughborough Road (two photos above: 2016 and c1905).

The Crown & Anchor, 246 Brixton Road was built in c1880. It has a narrow but well composed four-storey façade with projecting ground-floor pub frontage which has a long side return on the short stretch of Ingleton Street, that survived the demolition of this road to create Slade Gardens in 1962. The pedimented central gable is flanked by a pair of urns. Below the dentil cornice are inscribed symbols of a crown and an anchor. Photos above: 2016 and c1905.

Pubs of Herne Hill

The **Prince Regent, 69 Dulwich Road** in Herne Hill (top photos; the interior taken in 1972) was rebuilt in 1890 on the site of a much older tavern, seen in the middle view of c1880, not long before its redevelopment. The late-Victorian successor is a confident essay in striped red brick and stone (the so-called streaky bacon or banded style) with a steep, almost vertically pitched fish-scale mansard, pedimented brick dormers and a statue within a niche below the gable. It is locally listed.

The Florence (originally the **Railway Tavern** and by 1900 renamed the **Brockwell Park Hotel**), **131-133 Dulwich Road**, opened in 1867, just five years after the railway arrived in Herne Hill (bottom view). Its two street elevations have Italianate detailing to the bracketed eaves and pedimented window surrounds. The pub front is tiled in a honey-coloured faience. It is also locally listed.

There are many more fine pubs in Herne Hill and West Dulwich, all covered in much greater detail in the excellent book *'The Pubs of Dulwich & Herne Hill'* by the Dulwich Society and the Herne Hill Society published in 2016.

Pubs of Clapham, Stockwell and Wandsworth Road

The Bread and Roses (originally the **Bowyer Arms**), **68 Clapham Manor Street** has been a very popular local hostelry since it was built in 1852 as part of Thomas Cubitt's development of the district (top photo). It is a dignified three-storey building of stock brick with stucco window surrounds and an imposing central porch (originally open, later in-filled to create a lobby) adorned with a pair of pineapple finials, a haulingway to the right accessing the rear yard and glazed brown tiles to the ground floor, again added later. The middle photo of this Grade II listed building was taken in 1909.

The Railway Tavern (now simply **The Railway**), **18 Clapham High Street**, is the end of a short terrace of three-storey mid-Victorian properties built in 1868 (bottom left photo). The locally listed building has a semi-circular pediment on the canted corner and an attractive pub frontage.

The Bobbin, 1-3 Lillieshall Road, Clapham was formerly named the Tim Bobbin (bottom right photo) and was designed by B. Elson in 1887. The red brick upper-storey has a dentil cornice, modillions terminating the slender pilasters and ornate iron balconettes. The

ground floor has a traditional timber pub front with four plate glass sash windows. It is Grade II listed.

The Alexandra Hotel, 14 Clapham Common Southside (top photo) forms the centrepiece of a Grade II listed trio of properties designed by noted architect Edward l'Anson (President of the Royal Institute of British Architects in 1886) whose work included several important buildings in the City of London including the Merchant Taylors' Hall. The five-storey hotel was built in 1863 and has a grand façade of stock brick with polychrome brick dressings, topped by a fish-scale slated mansard and dome. Bottom left photo: 1965.

The Two Brewers, 114 Clapham High Street (middle photo below) is one of the longest established gay venues in London, serving the community since the 1980s. The pub itself dates back a further 120 years to c1860 - it has simple elevations of stock brick and a stuccoed parapet and window architraves. A Greek key motif runs along the string course above the fascia.

The Sun, 47 Old Town in Clapham (bottom right photo) was rebuilt in c1880 replacing an older hostelry on this site. It has a plain façade of stock brick with red brick pilasters, string courses and window surrounds, a projecting pub front with urns above the large console brackets at each end. The roof is crowned by a French-style slated turret with a decorative iron balustrade.

The Marquis of Lorne, 49 Dalyell Road on the corner of Combermere Road in Stockwell is a Grade II listed building dating from c1880 (top two photos). The upper storeys are of stock brick with stucco quoins and terracotta arched window surrounds, their deep reveals decorated with foliate leaf patterns. It has an outstanding ground floor façade of green, gold and brown glazed tiles with arabesque patterns on the pilasters seen in the middle photo.

The Surprise, 16 Southville (bottom left) between Larkhall Park and Wandsworth Road is a real gem of a small traditional pub, locally listed, built in c1860. It has a timber pub front and trio of classically detailed windows and simple cornice above.

The Priory Arms, 83 Lansdowne Way in Stockwell has a fine corner frontage with hand-painted signage and elegant pilasters. Its wrap-around fascia is festooned with hanging baskets. Built in c1865, it is locally listed (middle photo below).

The Mawbey Arms, 7 Mawbey Street (bottom right) is a charming pub of c1860, the sole survivor from a 1970s council redevelopment scheme to build the Mawbey Estate. Locally listed, it has a fine painted timber pub front and corner lantern.

The former **Bell, 274 Wandsworth Road** (now a shop and flats) is a stately composition dating from 1860 (top photo). The locally listed three-storey building has elevations of stock brick with red brick and stone dressings, charming bell and fan motifs over the first floor windows and a projecting ground-floor pub frontage surmounted by a balustrade. Sadly the pub front was stripped out after its closure in 2007.

The Grosvenor (formerly **Grosvenor Arms), 17 Sidney Road** in Stockwell was built in c1865 (bottom left) and regrettably closed in 2014. It has been gutted internally but retains its attractive mid-Victorian exterior.

The former **Victoria Tavern, 642 Wandsworth Road** (below right) was built in c1860, it closed in 2014. It has a brick façade with stucco dressings including quoins, and a good pub front with polished granite pilasters. It is locally listed.

Pubs of Norwood, Tulse Hill and West Dulwich

The Tulse Hill Hotel, 150 Norwood Road (top photo) occupies a commanding position at the junction of what is now the South Circular. It was built in c1845 as the Tulse Hill Tavern but had assumed its present name by the time the middle left photo was taken in 1891. Its London stock brick elevations with its name incised in a stucco band at high level and hipped slate roof have changed little over the years. It is locally listed and has recently been restored as a fine hotel and restaurant. It is pictured below in 1965.

The former **White Swan Hotel** (now the **Westow House**), **79 Westow Hill**, marks the gateway into Lambeth from the boroughs of Bromley, Southwark and Croydon. The earlier Swan tavern was rebuilt in c1875 and has an Italianate façade of stock brick with classical stucco window pediments (bottom photo). The pub frontage has rusticated paired pilasters and a modillion cornice. The locally listed building lost its second floor in c1960 following damage in the Second World War. This popular local landmark would greatly benefit from its reinstatement.

The Paxton Hotel, 255 Gipsy Road, is a distinctive landmark at the bottom of Gipsy Hill (top photos - left view: c1905.). This locally listed building of c1855 has a three-storey tower with a pyramidal roof and Italianate detailing, particularly the handsome bracketed eaves. It was named after the architect of the Crystal Palace, Sir Joseph Paxton.

The Rosendale Hotel (now **The Rosendale**), **66 Rosendale Road** stands at the junction of Park Hall Road. The Grade II listed pub (middle photo) was built in c1860. It has stuccoed upper elevations and a ground floor clad with a rich brown faience added in c1900. Grand porches on both frontages have elegant composite columns.

The Norwood Hotel, 3 Knight's Hill (now called **The Great North Wood**) is a noble mid-Victorian Jacobean-style public house built of red brick with stucco dressings including unusual semi-circular ended quoins (bottom photo). Built in c1865, it has a stuccoed ground-floor frontage with arched windows divided by pilasters. Arched and pedimented parapet dormers grace the roofline but sadly the tall needle and ball finials on the ridge have been lost. It is also locally listed.

Halfway up Gipsy Hill (no.79) stands the much larger **Gipsy Hill Tavern**, built in c1865 (photos below and top left, the latter taken in c1970). It is a fine example of mid-Victorian Italianate pub architecture with a symmetrical upper façade of gault brick and stucco dressings with deep bracketed eaves. The entablature of the imposing columned porch also forms the fascia and modillion cornice to the pub front. An equally grand return elevation welcomes potential punters emerging from the railway station immediately to the north. It is locally listed.

The Railway Bell, 14 Cawnpore Street stands on a quiet side road leading off Gipsy Hill (bottom left view). It was opened in 1892 and can be seen on the right-hand side of the street in the middle left photo taken in c1920 looking east towards the monumental Crystal Palace erected in 1852 (which burnt down in 1936) as a backdrop. This modest locally listed pub has a traditional painted timber pub frontage with a projecting signboard, and a popular beer garden.

Pubs of Streatham

The Leigham Arms, 1-3 Wellfield Road (top photo and middle view of 1968) is an attractive locally listed hostelry dating from 1860. It is a modest country village-style pub built of stuccoed blockwork with a simple frontage, the leaded light windows set between unadorned piers, the canted corner facing the junction with Sunnyhill Road. Its rural character is reinforced by the traditional post mounted painted pub sign.

The Horse & Groom, 60 Streatham High Road (bottom left) was rebuilt in 1865, replacing an earlier 18th century tavern said to have been frequented by the Prince Regent (later George IV) for gambling on his way to Brighton. It was previously known as the **Halfway House** since it stands about half way between London and Croydon. The locally listed building is built of brick (over-painted in c2000) with shallow arches above the windows, a central pointed gable and gabled dormers. The photo below right was taken in c1885 and shows a London to Redhill and Brighton stagecoach waiting outside. The golden age of stage coaches had long been eclipsed by this time following the opening of the London to Brighton railway in 1841 but a much reduced service still operated until the advent of the first motor coach service in 1905.

The White Lion, 232-234 Streatham High Road
was rebuilt in 1895 to a design by F. Gough & Co of
Hendon. It replaced a far more modest 18th or early
19th century hostelry - the two-storey stucco fronted
building with a pediment to the left of the horse-drawn
omnibus in the top photo below taken in c1890.

It is of a grandiose Flemish style with a splendid
façade of red brick with stone dressings, three highly
elaborate shaped gables topped with stone pinnacle
finials, two octagonal chimneystacks either side of the
central pediment above a first and second floor oriel
bay and canted first-floor windows set within deep
ached reveals.

It also has an increasingly rare original ground floor
frontage of polished pink and grey granite pilasters,
composite capitals, panelled stallrisers and timber
glazing bars. The lower two-storey left hand wing
had a haulingway for deliveries to the rear of the
pub (recently infilled) and still has an elegant curved
shopfront. The bottom left photo was taken in c1902
with Streatham Tate Library in the background, a
recent photo is bottom right. It is locally listed but
is of such exceptional quality that it surely deserves
adding to the National Heritage List.

The Railway, 2 Greyhound Lane (top photo) was built in c1875 a few years after what was originally named Greyhound Lane station opened on the opposite side of the road in 1862 (renamed Streatham Common station in 1870). It has unpretentious façades of stock brick with stucco surrounds to the arched windows to the first floor and flattened arched windows on the top floor. The middle photo shows the pub and the very genteel-looking parade of gabled shops opposite in 1912.

The former Bedford Park Hotel, 233 Streatham High Road (bottom left photo) erected in 1882 sadly succumbed to the recent wave of pub closures and shut in 2009. It has a half-timbered and gabled oriel perched high on the façade above one of a pair of double-height canted bay windows. Slender tiled roofed porches bearing *Saloon* lettering shelter the two entrances. It is now a shop. The photo below shows the pub in 1903 on the right, with the spire of Streatham Methodist Church in the background, demolished in 1967 (see entry on page 180 in the Lost Lambeth chapter).

HOUSING

At the beginning of Queen Victoria's reign in 1837 Lambeth was still predominantly rural to the south of the Oval, comprising linear development along all of the main arteries (mostly in the form of villas and Georgian terraced houses) linking up with the settlements of Clapham and Stockwell and extending like tentacles as far as Balham, Brixton Hill, Tulse Hill and Herne Hill. Streatham and Norwood were still separate villages surrounded by fields and woods. By the 1870s the built-up area had reached Brixton (see map on page 6) and by the end of her reign, Lambeth was virtually fully developed with only a few pockets of land still awaiting development. The enormous rise in the capital's population, the rapid growth of an affluent middle class seeking attractive new homes with gardens in the suburbs and the equally rapid construction of a highly developed system of public transport (suburban railways, trams and buses) ensured this transformation of the borough.

This chapter will assess some examples of housing built during these 64 years, showcasing the most interesting developments on a geographical basis starting in North Lambeth and moving south.

Housing North Lambeth and Kennington

Walcot Square (bottom left photo) and **St Mary's Gardens** (bottom right photo) were laid out by the Walcot Estate in 1837-39, both comprising green triangular 'squares' enclosed by railings overlooked by two- and three-storey terraced houses of stock brick, sash windows with flat gauged brick arches and simple stucco surrounds to the front doors in the Georgian tradition. All the original houses are Grade II listed and remarkably well preserved by virtue of careful management by the Walcot Estate including replica reconstruction following damage in the Second World War, a very early conservation area designation (in 1968) and listing in 1981.

The **White House, 54 Kennington Oval** (top view), is a fine early-Victorian residence built in the c1840s which was once the vicarage to St Mark's Church. Stucco fronted with a Gothic-style gabled porch and a hipped slated roof, this Grade II listed building was the birthplace of Field Marshal Montgomery of Alamein (1897-1976) who commanded the British Eighth Army in North Africa and Italy during the Second World War. **Hanover Gardens** (middle photo) is a secluded square laid out in the late 1840s by the Islington builder, John Glenn who also developed Albert Square. The two- and three-storey terraces of stock brick fronted houses (all Grade II listed) have margin-pane sash windows and simple stuccoed entablature surrounds to the front doors.

Cleaver Square (bottom left) was laid out in the Georgian period in the 1790s to 1830s but a few plots remained to be filled and in c1850 the architect William Rogers of Palace Chambers, Old Lambeth, built **21-25** and **26-33** which are more elaborate than their earlier neighbours with stucco quoins and window pediments, console bracketed dentil courses and rusticated ground floors (Grade II listed). The locally listed **59 Kennington Road**, originally on Wolsingham Place, has a fine curved façade of c1860 with Tudor-style porches and hood moulds over the windows (photo below).

MODEL HOUSES FOR FOUR FAMILIES,

ERECTED AT THE CAVALRY BARRACKS, HYDE PARK,

IN CONNEXION WITH

THE EXPOSITION OF THE WORKS OF INDUSTRY OF ALL NATIONS, 1851,

BY

HIS ROYAL HIGHNESS PRINCE ALBERT, K.G.,

PRESIDENT OF THE SOCIETY FOR IMPROVING THE CONDITION OF THE LABOURING CLASSES.

A   Sink, with Coal Box under.
B   Plate Rack over entrance to Dust Shaft, D.
C   Meat Safe, ventilated through hollow bricks.
E   Staircase of Slate, with Dust Place under.
F   Cupboard warmed from back of Fireplace.
G   Linen Closet in this recess if required.

Scale of .... feet.

The Prince Consort Lodge has stood on the western edge of **Kennington Park** since it was re-erected here in 1852 after being on display as a Model Dwelling at the Great Exhibition in Hyde Park in 1851. It was commissioned by the Society for Improving the Condition of the Labouring Classes of which Queen Victoria's consort, Prince Albert was president. Designed by architect Henry Roberts it cost less than £460 to build. The two-storey Grade II listed building of stock brick with red brick bands and window headers comprised four flats, each with a living room, three bedrooms, a scullery and a lavatory (see front elevation and floor plan to left). The covered staircase at the front accessed the two upper flats. For maximum fire-proofing only brick and concrete (no wood) were used in its construction. It was very influential on the improved housing for the working classes which followed. It became the home and offices of the park superintendent, and is now the offices for the organisation Trees for Cities.

The small neighbourhood of four streets in the heart of Kennington known as the **East Estate** (named after the landowner who developed this land in the early 1870s, Sir Gilbert East) is a very well preserved example of high-density middle class housing from this era (top photo: **Methley Street**). Alfred Lovejoy designed the attractive two- and three-storey terraced houses above semi-basements with attractive polychromatic brick elevations on a grid plan (see the plan published in the 1956 Survey of London).

Pictured below is another very fine example of mid-Victorian Gothic Revival architecture in Kennington - the **Old Vicarage, 94 Lambeth Road** which dates from c1880. It is a pleasing composition of stock brick with red brick dressings, an exceptionally good gabled stone porch supported on grand composite columns and very fine and rare wrought iron railings. It is locally listed but surely deserves a Grade II designation.

The Peabody Trust laid out the **Stamford Street Estate** of 352 dwellings in 16 blocks in 1875 with four more blocks added in the 1890s (top photos: 2016 and c1905). Four blocks (C, D, V and U) were demolished in the c1970s to create more open space when the flats were also modernised internally. A successful environmental project in the 1990s included the soft landscaping of the grounds around the austere blocks. Peabody's architect at the time was Henry Astley Darbishire (1825-99). They were so well built they have outlived many more recent housing estates.
The blocks have slate roofs and huge chimneys. The elevations of yellow London stock brick are articulated by bands of white Suffolk brick with terracotta lintels and cornices, and have imposing porches of rusticated stucco.

St Olave's House on **Walnut Tree Walk** in Kennington (bottom photo) is another example of later Victorian social (then known as philanthropic) housing. The 16 tenement flats within the four-storey frontage block are accessed via staircases at the rear. It was built in 1884 and has a finely crafted façade with segmental arched windows and a central arched entrance to the passageway to the rear, enlivened by classically inspired modillions and keystones. The scheme included a row of two-storey dwellings to the rear (1-11 St Olave's Gardens) which were reconstructed in 2003. This type of block dwelling was relatively common in inner London but so many have been demolished since the 1960s they are now quite rare. It is locally listed.

Housing in Vauxhall

Bonnington Square (top photo) was laid out in 1881 and soon housed railway employees working at the nearby Nine Elms Goods Yard. Threatened with demolition to make way for a new school in the 1980s, it was 'squatted' and became a housing cooperative with a vegetarian cafe and community garden. Lambeth declared it part of the Vauxhall Conservation Area in 1984 and its attractive yellow brick properties are now in good order.

Rowton House (now the **Centrepoint Soho Vauxhall Hostel**), **11 Bondway** (middle photo) was the first of the philanthropist Lord Rowton's model lodging houses for working class men. Designed by Harry Bell Measures, it opened in 1892, it was renovated in 1974 to provide 150 bedsits. Its symmetrical five-storey façade is of stock and red brick dressings with an imposing central entrance portico.

Park Mansions (bottom photos: 2016 and 1912) on **South Lambeth Road** overlooks Vauxhall Park. It is a five-storey block of 50 flats built in 1894. It has well detailed red brick elevations incorporating elegant gables, bay windows, a corner entrance bay, mansard roofs and tall chimneys.

Victoria Mansions and **Victoria House** is a huge late-Victorian block of flats on **South Lambeth Road** erected in c1895, (top photo and seen in the background of the c1920 middle photo which also shows the bustling street life of this thoroughfare with its parades of shops). It has tall red brick elevations like cliff faces, the brick was recently cleaned revealing its handsome appearance long hidden by pollution. At its southern apex it is terminated by a clay-tiled conical turret. It formed a group with Albert and Atholl Mansions directly opposite until their demolition in 1975. See their Lost Lambeth entry on page 207.

Shaftesbury House and **Cromwell House** on **Vauxhall Walk** are a pair of five-storey blocks of 20 walk-up tenement flats built in c1890 (bottom left view). Their once open staircases were designed to allow maximum ventilation. **Oval Mansions** on **Kennington Oval** (bottom right photo) date from c1890 and is another good example of this building type, notable for its cast iron window pediments and its restoration in recent years.

Housing in South Lambeth

South Lambeth retains a wealth of Victorian heritage, protected by a number of conservation areas designated since the 1960s. **106-112 Fentiman Road** (top photo) date from c1840. They are two pairs of semi-detached three-storey townhouses faced with stucco with incised lines to resemble blocks of stone (Grade II).

Immediately to the west are the **Noel Caron Almshouses, 1-7 Fentiman Road** (middle photo - Grade II) which were originally established on what is now the Wandsworth Road in 1618 but relocated here in 1854. They have warm red elevations with three-light casement windows set in stone surrounds, with Tudor-arched heads to the ground floor. A central shaped gable stands over a gabled porch.

Richborne Terrace (bottom left view) was built in the 1850s. It was originally named Richmond Terrace on the north side and Osborne Terrace on the south. Neither are listed. Both terraces comprise over 30 properties on a scale more common in Belgravia or Pimlico sharing a uniform design of rusticated stucco raised ground-floor and semi-basement elevations and stock brick above. They have semi-circular or triangular pediments to the grand piano nobile (first floor). Over a third of Richmond Terrace was destroyed during the Second World War and on the site of nos. 34-62 a row of 12 'prefabs' were built. These were replaced by a new block of council maisonettes by the LCC in 1958 which echo the parapet height and building line of the original terrace. It is faced with a similar stock brick and render palette of materials albeit to a 1950s design. It is an interesting reinterpretation of the 1850s architectural form a century on.

Claylands Road, **Trigon Road** (top photo) and **Meadow Road** to the north of Fentiman Road date from the 1850s and were also spared post-war redevelopment. They have been protected within a conservation area since 1969 but are unlisted. They are of a modest scale - two storeys, some above semi-basements, with simple façades of stock brick and stucco window and door surrounds. They have London roofs (also called butterfly or valley roofs - gutters running front to back) concealed behind front parapets above a simple cornice.

Albert Square (middle view) is arguably the grandest set-piece 19th century square in Lambeth. It was laid out by the Islington builder John Glenn from 1846. It has a broad tree-lined approach from Clapham Road and very substantial houses of five floors grouped in a formal symmetrical fashion, in pairs or trios, linked at raised ground-floor level by entrance porches. They are of an unmistakably early-Victorian classical design embellished with stucco dressings, elegant balustrades, quoins and dentil cornices. All are Grade II listed.

South Lambeth Road is lined with many fine later Georgian and Victorian homes. **No. 261 (Wingfield House** - bottom photo) is perhaps the most imposing with its grand façade of stock brick decorated with rusticated quoins, classical triangular and semi-circular pediments over the windows and an impressive rusticated porch, all in stucco. It forms part of the second phase of development of this road in the 1840s-60s, following an initial phase between the 1790s and 1830s. The simplicity of the earlier late-Georgian houses gave way to a rich variety of neo-classical and Italianate influences exhibited here at Wingfield House. Most are locally listed.

On the borders of South Lambeth and Stockwell lies another elegant piece of early-Victorian town planning with a formal circus at its centre - **Lansdowne Gardens**, laid out by John Snell between 1843 and 1870. Enclosing the circular garden are quadrants of three-storey houses (top right photo) which divide axial streets of three- and four-storey properties. They are of a variety of designs but all share the same classical vocabulary of columned porches, Grecian-style pilasters, moulded cornices and architraves. They have modest front gardens enclosed by railings and generous rear gardens.

The vista up one axis (St Barnabas Villas) is terminated by the Church of St Barnabas completed in 1850 (see page 145). The neighbourhood has been protected by one of Lambeth's earliest conservation area designations since 1968, the year after the Civic Amenities Act was passed, the piece of legislation which introduced this form of heritage protection. The top left view shows a semi-detached pair of houses on **Guildford Road**, the middle view is of the Jacobean-style gabled **Mandragon House** (formerly the vicarage, c1850) and the bottom photo is of **St Barnabas Villas**. Many but by no means all of these houses are Grade II listed.

Housing in Stockwell

1-8 Stockwell Terrace (top photo) front what remains of the once far more extensive Stockwell Common, now a triangular public open space containing the distinguished war memorial clock tower of 1921. The refined façades have rusticated stucco raised ground floors, with slated mansard roofs and dormers. Full width balconies have patterned cast iron railings. The Grade II listed terrace was built in 1843.

Stockwell Park is one of the largest and most complete early-Victorian neighbourhoods in Lambeth, protected by its own conservation area since 1968. It possesses a wide variety of house types - detached and semi-detached villas and terraces sitting in verdant gardens and on tree-lined streets. The suburb was laid out between the two Roman roads, Brixton Road and Clapham Road which by the 1830s were already lined with large townhouses. **Stockwell Park Road** is the meandering spine of the suburb off which runs the gracefully curving **Stockwell Park Crescent** (seen in the recent middle photo and the bottom photo taken in c1912) and the linear roads of Groveway and Lorn Road which link it with Brixton Road. They were mainly developed in the 1840s and have a very arcadian and spacious character.

The variety of architectural styles delight the eye ranging from simple neo-classical and Italianate elements combining stock brick and stucco, to the picturesque Gothick style on Lorn Road and even Queen Anne and Arts and Crafts of the late-Victorian period on the northern part of Stockwell Park Road. About one third are listed Grade II - more deserve to be.

Top photo: **Lorn Road**'s outstanding Grade II listed Victorian Gothick villas (c1843 - note the steeply pitched gables adorned with fancy bargeboards, the battlemented parapets and pointed arch porches); Middle photos: the stately Italianate villas on **Groveway** in c1905 (when it was still named Grove Road) and 2016; and bottom photos: **Durand Gardens** in 2016 and c1912 - a wonderful oasis between two busy arterial roads – early-Victorian detached and semi-detached houses grouped around a tree-lined residents' square, including these unusual bow-fronted villas with classical porches and deep overhanging eaves.

Housing in Clapham

Clapham was already well-established as a prosperous residential district when Victoria ascended the throne in 1837. Wealthy merchants had built large villas there since the late 17th century and by the 1830s it was served by regular horse-drawn omnibus services to the City and West End. Thomas and William Cubitt developed vast tracts of land between 1825 and the 1850s, creating the arcadian suburb of Clapham Park and more modest houses around Clapham Manor Street. The opening of Clapham station (now Clapham High Street station) in 1862 and the arrival of the first tram in 1871 further accelerated its growth. The top two photos are of **Grafton Square** (middle view: c1860), which was constructed in 1846-51 by Thomas Ross, but only two-and-a-half sides were built to his proposed layout. They are tall and gracious stucco fronted terraced townhouses enjoying a fine aspect over the garden square. The **Hibbert Almshouses, 715-729 Wandsworth Road** (bottom left) were built in 1858 in the Gothic style by sisters Sarah and Mary Ann Hibbert in memory of their father William Hibbert. **Linton House, 54 Clapham Common Southside** (below) is a handsome detached classical villa of 1875 with a grand balustraded Corinthian portico. All are Grade II listed.

43-47 and **49-52 Clapham Common Northside** are a pair of French Renaissance-style terraces fronting Clapham Common, each comprise five seven-storey townhouses. Known as **Cedars Terraces**, these impressive landmark buildings were designed by James Knowles and completed in 1860, two years before his palatial Grosvenor Hotel opened next to Victoria Station. Grade II listed, they are of an attractive gault brick with stucco dressings and continuous cast iron balcony to the third floors. The bottom photo shows the terraces in 1866.

The pair form bookends to Cedars Road, reinforced by their end pavilions which have very tall slate mansard roofs topped by ornate ironwork. Immense chimneys punctuate the roofline. Knowles also laid out the Park Town Estate, less than a mile to the north either side of Queenstown Road in Battersea.

Pictured here are just a few of the many fine Victorian residences built in Clapham between 1860 and 1900. **113-119 Cedars Road** (top view, Grade II listed) by J.T. Knowles are the only three of the 35 villas to survive the destruction of the Second World War only to be razed by LCC planners in the early 1960s to create the Cedars Road housing estate. **The Chase** retains almost all of its Dutch gabled villas of the 1870s (middle left) and Arts and Crafts-style red brick gabled and canted bay-windowed houses built in 1887 (middle right).The northern third of **Victoria Rise**, laid out in c1875, survived the post-war clearances (bottom photos, right view dating from 1914).

In addition to the grand tree-lined avenues of three- and four-storey townhouses, Clapham also has a multitude of more modest streets of terraced Victorian housing. The top photo shows a wonderfully embellished end of terrace at **6 Haselrigge Road** (locally listed) erected in 1871 with a corner turret crowned by a spire and also a belvedere, richly decorated fish-scale slate roofs and polychromatic brickwork. The **Sibella Road** Conservation Area in North Clapham (bottom left) has a wealth of fine terraced homes

designed in an eclectic mix of architectural styles by E.B. l'Anson in the 1870s.

Only the southern half of the imposing French Renaissance-style **Carlton Mansions, 380-382 Clapham Road** survives following the loss of the northern half in the 1950s. It was built in c1877 (photo left). The bottom right view is the very characterful gault brick artisan housing on **Rectory Gardens** built in 1882.

East of Clapham Common lies the Grade II listed **78 Clapham Common Southside** (1888 - top photo). It forms a gateway to the attractive red brick terraces in the Abbeville Road neighbourhood that were largely built between the 1870s and 1890s. One by one, the huge old houses standing in extensive grounds were demolished in this period and replaced by a grid of streets of terraced housing such as **Elms Road** (middle photo - properties built by Charles Leathley in 1884), their façades enlivened with bay windows, polychromatic brickwork and stucco porches.

Further east lay the mid-19th century neighbourhood of large villas laid out by Thomas Cubitt forming **Clapham Park**. Very few of these grand detached residences survived the Second World War and the mass clearance in the 1940s and 50s by the LCC to build the vast Clapham Park Estate (see *Lambeth Architecture 1945-65*) but a few grand brick and/or stucco houses of the early Victorian era remain on **Atkins Road**, **Thornton Road** and **King's Avenue** (two examples pictured below - both are Grade II listed).

Housing in Brixton and West Camberwell

This area has a great legacy of Victorian housing notwithstanding huge losses in the 1960s and 70s. In 1837 settlement was confined to 'ribbon development' of large villas lining Brixton Road, Effra Road and Brixton Hill with cottages along Coldharbour Lane, Acre Lane and Loughborough Road. By 1860 development was surging ahead as the estates of villas in Angell Town and Loughborough Park were well underway and more modest housing was beginning to be built, a trend accelerated by the arrival of the railways in the early 1860s. One of the finest examples is the Grade II listed **Angell Terrace, 341-361 Brixton Road** (photos right: 2016 and 1898) built in 1860-68 by the builder James Barker of Peckham. It is of a palatial 'Kensington' scale, of a classical design with fine stuccowork, quoins, Roman Doric porches and a festooned and bracketed cornice surmounted by elegant urns.

On the Camberwell border the **Myatt's Fields** neighbourhood was developed by the Minet Family in the decades following the opening of Camberwell and Loughborough Junction stations in 1862-64. Gracious red brick villas and mansion blocks were built in the streets in the vicinity of Myatt's Fields Park, St James's Church and the Minet Library, all provided by the Minets. Bottom photos: **Knatchbull Road** in c1905 and **Burton House** (14 flats) on **Brief Street** built in 1893 (locally listed).

The Female Friendly Society was founded in 1802 for *'the relief of aged women'* living within ten miles of St Paul's. It built a range of almshouses in Camberwell in 1823 and then these at **155-167 Stockwell Park Road** in 1863 (top photo and middle lithograph of c1865). Originally seven in number, the three cottages at the southern end were lost in 1941 during the Blitz, rebuilt in 1948 and recently demolished. The **Friendly Almshouses** comprise three short two-storey terraces with attractive yellow brick elevations adorned with orange brick window and door surrounds, diaper brickwork at first floor and charmingly rustic timber porches on elongated brackets and topped by spike finials. The front gardens are enclosed by a dwarf wall and original cast iron railing.

Angell Town was a fashionable and well-planned residential quarter of large villas to the east of Brixton Road laid out in the 1850s. Most were demolished in the 1970s to create Lambeth's Angell Town estate but a stately row of Italianate detached and paired villas on the gracefully curving **St John's Crescent** survives (bottom view). They are of stock brick with grand classical stucco porches and window surrounds, and have shallow hipped slate roofs and bracketed eaves. Others survive on Wiltshire Road.

Loughborough Park is a well-planned and gracious middle class suburb laid out in the 1840s when the landowner, Lady Holland began granting building leases on what were pastures and market gardens. Broad tree-lined avenues of detached and paired houses were built with classical detailing in the Regency or Italianate style, set back behind spacious front gardens (top and bottom left photos). About half of the villas survived the demolitions of the 1960s by Lambeth Council to build the Moorlands Estate and create the Loughborough Park open space. In 1981 over 30 houses were Grade II listed and the remaining properties on Moorland Road, Loughborough Park and Coldharbour Lane were protected by a conservation area. The middle view is of Loughborough Park in 1921.

Pictured below is a good example of a Venetian Gothic-style house on **Akerman Road (no.56)** with a raised ground floor, polychromatic brickwork and an unusual recessed porch. It was the home of the music hall star Dan Leno (1860-1904) who is commemorated by a blue plaque on the façade. The house is locally listed.

Ferndale Road was designed by the architect Thomas Collcutt (who also designed the Imperial Institute in Kensington, the Savoy Hotel and the Palace Theatre), and laid out in the 1870s by the builder Josiah George Jennings. Jennings was also a noted sanitary engineer who invented the first public flush toilet and underground public lavatory. The townscape has survived remarkably complete. The three- and four-storey terraces of grey brick are embellished with a riot of the then newly-fashionable terracotta detailing manufactured by Jennings' company including vermiculated quoins, decorative eave brackets, string courses and door and window head (top photo).

At the western end of the Jennings' Estate is the Jacobean-influenced **Rathcoole House** (1882, bottom right photo - note its richly decorated elliptical oriel bay window) and the five-storey **53-63 Bedford Road** which is the grandest terrace of the development. At the eastern end is a small group of shops (**118-120 Ferndale Road** are pictured bottom left). All of the above are Grade II listed.

Also on **Ferndale Road** lie the **City of London Almshouses** which replaced earlier ones erected in 1836 built *"to afford a permanent asylum to aged and decayed freeman and householders of London, and their wives or widows, of good character and repute,..."* (a quote from a Corporation of London document of 1834 in the Guildhall Library). The dwellings face a central landscaped quadrangle. The **Rogers' Almshouses** (1860, top left view) at the northern end of the east side are of stock brick with gables and are Gothic in style. The single-storey **Gresham Almshouses** (1888, top right) at the southern end of the east side have a Jacobean influence. They are both Grade II listed. The locally listed two-storey **Freemen's Almshouses** to the west and south of 1885 are flats (middle photo). They are of red brick with stone dressings, a galleried first floor and pavilions with short towers at each end.

Trinity Gardens (bottom photo) is an appealing square lined on three sides by early-Victorian terraced houses set back with pretty front gardens, and a corner pub (the Trinity Arms, see page 92) all erected in the 1840s. They are of stock brick with simple stucco bands and surrounds to the sash windows, their 'London roofs' hidden by parapets (locally listed). The south side was pulled down in c1952 to build Daisy Dormer Court.

Three very different blocks of Victorian flats in Brixton are pictured here (all locally listed). **Dover Mansions, Canterbury Crescent** (top) is a grandiose Queen Anne-style red brick block of 1890 with Dutch gables built by the Minet Estate, which would look equally at home in Chelsea. **Carlton Mansions, 387 Coldharbour Lane** (bottom left) by G. Warren Cooper is a Jacobean-style mansion block of 1890 with a multi-pilastered red brick and stone façade on a long, slender site. The **St George's Residences, 80 Railton Road** (below), is an unusual and early block of artisan flats built in 1878. It has a square tower over the entrance (with circular windows) supporting a giant water tank and an L-shaped block of balcony-access flats behind.

Mayall Road is a good example of a mid-Victorian street of terraced housing built in 1871-76. Its beautiful polychromatic brickwork can be appreciated in the top photo of c1905 and recent middle left view. At the northern end of **St Matthew's Road** is the late Victorian Gothic-style **Baltic House** by Beazley & Burrows (c1885, photo below, locally listed) once the Brixton National Schools and then a Girls' Friendly Society hostel. The long terraces of three-storey red brick, gabled houses on **Raleigh Gardens**, Brixton Hill were built in 1890 (bottom photos: 2016 and c1905).

The **Rush Common and Brixton Hill Conservation Area** designated in 1997 has a wealth of fine avenues to the east of the historic linear Rush Common (protected by the 1806 Inclosure Act) which span the whole Victorian era. **Archbishop's Place** is one of the earliest developments, its modest two-storey paired cottages in a simple vernacular style are set back behind cottage gardens (top view).

Elm Park was laid out gradually between the 1830s and the 1870s (photo below of c1921 and recent view bottom right). It exhibits a wonderful architectural range from Georgian-style terraces of stock brick with rusticated stucco ground floors at the western end, to more elaborate terraces of the 1860s with bay windows festooned with decorated stucco detailing. Then come three- to four-storey gault brick terraces erected in the 1870s centred on

the Elm Park Tavern and extending down **Leander Road** and **Medora Road** (bottom left photo of c1905). Note their imposing Gothic-style porches of polychromatic brickwork, ornate and decorated parapets and gables. Taller gabled houses with delicate iron finials terminate the gently curving terrace that comprises **79-119 Elm Park** and punctuate its central section. The end houses also had turreted towers, just one surviving at 1 Medora Road.

To the north of Elm Park, **Leander Road, Arodene Road** and **Helix Road** (pictured above in c1905) extend towards Helix Gardens and Josephine Avenue. Attractive terraces of two-storey houses were laid out between 1875 and 1895 following the sale of the Raleigh Hall estate. They are similar in scale and plan with long half-width rear projections, with a great variety of elevational design. Built of gault brick their façades are enlivened by red brick and stucco dressings, square or canted bay windows often with hipped bay roofs, Gothic or classical porches, and tall gable ends.

Josephine Avenue (c1872) is a particularly gracious thoroughfare (top left photo), the 1806 Act of Parliament protecting Rush Common requiring the builders to set the three-storey terraced townhouses behind verdant landscaping and access drives. The houses on **Helix Gardens**, built in the 1890s have Gothic arches above the first-floor windows filled with decorative vertical tile-hung panels. At the southern end of the conservation area is **Holmewood Gardens** (middle photo of c1905 and bottom view) laid out in the 1890s around a large triangular public open space.

Housing in Herne Hill

Until well after the opening of Herne Hill station in 1862, Herne Hill comprised just a line of villas climbing Denmark Hill and Herne Hill set amidst open fields. It developed rapidly between the railway and Brockwell Park but much more slowly east of the railway where it remained largely rural until the end of the century. Only a handful of the Georgian and early-Victorian developments survived the redevelopment of the 1930s to 1950s, one such example is the locally listed Italianate stuccoed pair at **10-12 Herne Hill** pictured top left dating from c1850.

Modest and well-built housing for the skilled working class was erected in the 1870s on the **Milkwood Estate** on Lowden, Milkwood and Poplar roads (photo below). The larger and more elaborate red brick terraced houses on **Gubyon Avenue** and **Fawnbrake Avenue** (bottom left view of c1907) and adjoining roads were built from the mid 1880s. The middle photo is of houses on **Rollscourt Avenue** showing their elegant Arts and Crafts-style front porches, elaborate capitals on the bay windows and bracked eaves.

The Cottage, 155 Norwood Road (top view: c1895 and middle left view) is quite unique to Lambeth. It was built in c1890 in a quintessentially Old English style. The half-timbered cottage has fanciful bargeboards, diamond-pane leaded windows and an oriel window. **Dulwich Road** (bottom left) and **Poet's Corner** (Chaucer, Spenser, Shakespeare and Milton roads - the latter seen below in c1905, houses on Chaucer Road bottom right) is a fine Victorian neighbourhood. It has a diverse collection of terraced and semi-detached homes on tree-lined streets built of polychromatic brick, the houses are influenced by Venetian, Gothic, classical and Romanesque styles.

Housing in West Dulwich, Tulse Hill and Norwood

At the beginning of Victoria's reign this area comprised open fields, commons, farms and hamlets, but a line of late-Georgian villas marching over Tulse Hill was a portent of the urbanisation that was swiftly to follow. By the 1860s the villas had reached Crown Point as West Norwood expanded on all sides of the cemetery established there in 1837. By the end of the century the district was almost entirely suburban. The bottom photo and the sketch show one of the very few large detached Victorian villas in Tulse Hill to survive the mass demolitions of the 1950s and 60s - **Carisbrooke, 49 Upper Tulse Hill** (c1860, Grade II listed), now flats.

West Norwood has two important Gothic-style houses. The first is **Dudley House** on **Clive Road** built in 1882 (Grade II, top photo) by Ralph Gardiner, a master plasterer whose work can also be admired at Dulwich College. The exterior and interior have a riot of rich detail. The middle photo is of the Grade II listed **Gothic Lodge** on **Idmiston Road** built in the 1870s by Charles Drake who was an early proponent of shuttered concrete housing construction (he also built the Concrete House at 549 Lordship Lane in East Dulwich). True to its name it has Gothic arched windows with picturesque fretted bargeboards.

The highly creative talents of Ernest George and Harold Peto produced an outstanding asymmetrical pair of Arts and Crafts houses at **4** and **6 Thornlaw Road** in **West Norwood** (1883 - Grade II, top view). Tile-hung with bands of plain and fancy tiles, the high pitched roofs are crowned with massive chimneys and both have characterful entrances. The front door to no. 6 is sheltered by a recessed porch with an elliptical arch and no. 4 has a tiled covered way to the street.

Another house built in the Arts and Crafts style is the locally listed **51 Lovelace Road** in Tulse Hill (middle photo). It has attractive pebbledash elevations, fine front door, delicate wrought iron brackets to the eaves and slender candlestick finials.

The semi-detached stucco fronted classical-style villas at **33-61 Park Hall Road** in West Dulwich (bottom right) were built in 1846-54. Close by are avenues of later Victorian semi-detached villas built in the 1880s and 1890s on **Rosendale, Carson, Eastmearn and Dalmore roads** (bottom left). The red and stock brick houses have a wealth of architectural decoration including floral capitals to pilasters and decorated bargeboards.

Bloom Grove in **West Norwood** (top left) is a fine enclave of locally listed semi-detached mid-Victorian Italianate-style houses with either tall arched dormers set within bracketed eaves or full height bay windows. They were built in the 1880s, grouped around a garden square.

Gipsy Hill was a rural district until the construction of the Crystal Palace in 1854 (see photo left taken in c1920 with Woodland Hill and Woodland Road in the foreground) and the opening of the railway station in 1856. Development followed with elegant classical terraces lining the steep hill in the 1860s and 1870s (photo above) and substantial terraces of brick villas built on side streets in the same period, typified by the handsome gabled and bay-windowed properties on **Woodland Road** and **Jasper Road** (bottom view).

Housing in Streatham

Park Hill is a substantial Grade II* listed mansion to the north of Streatham Common (converted to flats in 2001 with 49 houses built in the grounds). The bottom photos show the interior in c1920 and the exterior in 1998. Built in c1835, just before Victoria ascended the throne, its owner William Leaf added a number of structures in the early 1870s (all listed Grade II). These include the classical-style stuccoed lodge decorated with the Leaf family's monogram and motto '*Folium non defluet*' - meaning "T*he Leaf does not fall*" (top view and 1939 middle left photo) which has

guarded the grand gateway to the drive since 1870; a folly and a grotto (photo left) which is made of Pulhamite artificial stone. It resembles a gorge and includes a sunken pathway below an ornate footbridge and two caverns. The sugar magnate and founder of the Tate Gallery, Sir Henry Tate lived here from 1880 to 1899.

The semi-detached cottages on **Sunnyhill Road** (top photo, nos. 60-78 are locally listed) have a remarkably rustic character, more like a street in a village than a London suburb. The gabled stock brick houses date from the 1860s. **Flint Cottage** on **Mount Ephraim Lane** (photo below) has a similar vernacular quality with its elevations of knapped flint and fancy barge boards (Grade II listed). Two conservation areas at the southern and northern ends of **Leigham Court Road** protect the last remaining vestiges of its opulent Victorian character. The middle left view is one of a group at its southern end of five noble red brick detached villas (**nos. 286-294**) with Gothic porches and tall gables of c1890. At

the northern end an important group of villas from the Victorian era survive including the Italianate-style **no. 16** (**Woodlawns**, 1868 - photo below), **no. 49** which is inspired by both Gothic and classical influences (1866, bottom left) and the Arts and Crafts-style **no. 76** (The Grange) of 1883, extended in 1900 (all three are locally listed).

Norman Shaw is reputed to have designed the locally listed **5 Pendennis Road** (top photo), a fine Arts and Crafts-style detached house with tile-hung elevations and Gothic porch, built in 1873. **Hambly Mansions (412-416a Streatham High Road**, middle row views of 2016 and c1910) is a handsome locally listed trio of houses by Ernest George & Harold Peto built in 1877. It has three large gables faced with fish-scale hung tiles, windows set in deep reveals, tall chimney stacks and an oriel bay. Sadly its ground floor is much altered. **Palace Road** was one of the grandest residential streets in the borough, lined by large detached villas laid out by the Roupell family between the 1840s and 1890s. Many were demolished in the 1960s to make way for the GLC estate and private flats but some remain, **no. 38** is pictured bottom left. It is an imposing detached mid-Victorian villa which is locally listed.

Riggindale Road (bottom right photo), Thirlmere Road and adjacent avenues were developed in the 1880s and comprise large attractive semi-detached houses with generous gardens. They are rich in architectural detail exhibiting a strong Queen Anne stylistic influenced no doubt by Norman Shaw's slightly earlier garden suburb at Bedford Park in Turnham Green.

Telford Park is an attractive late-Victorian neighbourhood in Streatham Hill. It was once farmland owned by the Duke of Bedford and later the Telford family. It was developed between 1878 and 1882 by the developer Eliot Hanney working with the building firm Sutton & Dudley and the architect E.J. Tarver. Fine semi-detached and terraced homes in the Queen Anne style were built on tree-lined thoroughfares such as **Telford Avenue** (top photo), **Killieser Avenue** (middle photo dating from c1914), **Criffel Avenue** (bottom left view) and **Kirkstall Avenue** (photo bottom right).

The front elevations of houses on the estate are remarkable for their diversity, employing a wide range of architectural features such as Dutch gables, turrets, decorated brickwork, dentil courses, hanging tiles, pilasters, bay windows, stained glass and pedimented porches. The houses are set back behind front gardens and have deep plans. The residents had the benefit of the Telford Park Lawn Tennis Club, opened in 1880. It is the second oldest club in England after Wimbledon. Telford Avenue was designated a conservation area in 1994.

The Leigham Court Estate (known locally as the ABC Estate by virtue of its road names) in Streatham Hill was constructed by the Artisans' Labourers' and General Dwellings Company, who laid out a planned community on the 66 acre site between 1889 and the 1920s. It built nearly 1,000 houses, maisonettes and flats on a formal grid pattern of streets together with St Margaret's Church and shopping parades on Streatham Hill (middle photo). The architects were first Rowland Plumbe (1838-1919) who had worked on the same company's Noel Park Estate in Wood Green and a number of churches, then Harry Bell Measures (1862-1940) whose work included over a dozen London Underground stations and Rowton House in Vauxhall.

The bottom views date from 1912 and 1905. The architecture of the estate exhibits a Flemish influence using red, yellow and honey-coloured glazed bricks, clay tiles, terracotta mouldings and ornate ironwork. Dutch gables, Venetian windows and turrets create a rich townscape. The dwellings were carefully planned to maximise light and ventilation to every room. It was declared a conservation area in 1981. Photos below: c1910.

Self Contained Maisonnettes.   Houses.

CHURCHES

Lambeth has an outstanding collection of Victorian churches notwithstanding the lamentable loss of other exceptional examples in the post-war years - see the Lost Lambeth chapter. Its surviving ecclesiastical heritage is featured here in chronological order.

St Michael's, Stockwell Park Road is an unusual Early English Gothic design by William Rogers, consecrated in 1841. The Grade II listed church was reorientated in 1880 when the main entrance was moved from the west end facing a lane to Stockwell Park Crescent to the east end beneath the steeple, the altar making the opposite journey to the west end. At the same time the box pews and the west gallery were removed, and the organ was moved to the south aisle. The galleries are supported on slender iron columns and cranked iron beams. The vista up Lorn Road to the octagonal east tower with its spirelets, gabled sides and stone spire is particularly impressive.

The elevations are of yellow stock and buff coloured Suffolk brick with stone copings, cills, string courses, finials and other details. The engraving (left) dates from c1842 and the top photo is of c1920.

Christ Church, Christchurch Road in Streatham is a striking Grade I listed landmark on the South Circular Road. It was designed by James Wild (1814-92), who combined exotic Moorish, Egyptian, Venetian, Rundbogenstil (German) and early Christian elements to create this unique and most impressive composition built in 1841. The church has a basilical plan and is entered through a central double-height recessed porch with voussoirs of alternating red and stock brick in front of which stand a pair of tall gate pylons crowned with pyramidal caps. Above the entrance is a Star of David traceried window. At the south eastern end soars a 113 foot (34 metre) campanile in the style of St Mark's, Venice which has a pyramidal roof and three long narrow openings to the bell tower. The beautiful galleried interior, seen in this photo of 1932, has tall columns with galleries either side above paired pointed arches and an eastern apse decorated with wall paintings. The engraving above dates from 1841.

The **Church of St John the Evangelist** on **Clapham Road** is a fine Greek classical church built in 1842, designed by Thomas Marsh Nelson (c1817-84). It comprises a simple gault brick box with a grand five bay portico of hexastyle Ionic columns supporting the pediment, all in stucco. Sheltered by the portico are three doorways, the central one grander with a moulded architrave and console bracketed cornice. A crypt occupies the entire footprint of the church. The interior was reordered by T.J. Bailey (the School Board for London architect - see page 44) in 1883. It is Grade II listed. The photo below dates from c1910.

St. Barnabas Church Guildford Road South Lambeth.

The former **St Barnabas Church** (now **Ekarro House**), **49A Guildford Road** in Stockwell was designed by Isaac Clarke and James Humphreys and completed in 1850. It is Early English Gothic in style, built of Kentish ragstone with a tall gabled west front to the street, with a slender octagonal bell turret. It has a simple plan with a nave and six bays, a shallow apse at the east end. The church closed in 1978 and was converted to flats in c1985. The photo above of the interior was taken in c1970, the middle left photo dates from c1906.

The **Oddfellows Hall, 27 Belmont Close** in Clapham (bottom photo) was built as the Strict Ebenezer Chapel in 1852, and then occupied by the Wesleyans from 1861 until 1908 when it was bought by the Oddfellows Manchester Unity Friendly Society for their Pride of Clapham branch who still meet here. It is also occupied by the Shambala Meditation Centre. The Grade II listed building has a frontage of stock brick crowned by a pediment formed by a stucco moulding.

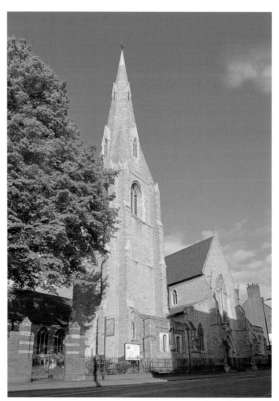

St Mary's Church (Our Lady of Victories) on **Clapham Park Road** is one of the finest Catholic churches in South London. It was completed in 1851 to a design by William Wardell (1824-99), with two chapels added in 1886 and 1895 by John Bentley (architect of Westminster Cathedral) who also designed the adjacent **Redemptorist Monastery** in 1893 (bottom right photo). The entire complex is Grade II* listed. The church is built of ragstone with freestone dressings in the 14th century style. Its splendid tower is a major local landmark. Bottom left photo: c1920.

St John's on **Wiltshire Road** in Brixton stands in the once-affluent neighbourhood of Angell Town. It was once surrounded by broad tree-lined avenues of substantial villas, but most were cleared in the 1970s to make way for the Angell Town Estate. The Grade II listed church was designed by Benjamin Ferrey (1810-80) in the Perpendicular Gothic style, faced in Kentish ragstone with Bath stone dressings. Its tall, imposing tower has chequered battlements of cream and grey ragstone and corner pinnacles. It was consecrated by the Bishop of Winchester in 1853.

A parish room was added to the north side of the chancel in 1882. Inside are two 1920s mosaics by local artist Gertrude Martin (bottom left and middle photos) in memory of her brothers Lawrence and George who were killed in the First World War. Her work can also be found in the cathedrals of Westminster and Belfast and in the Houses of Parliament. Top images: Photo c1905 and the original plan of 1853 from *The Builder*.

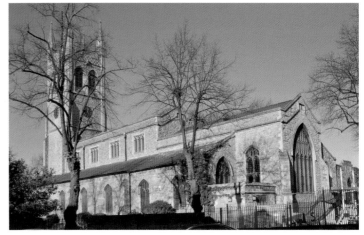

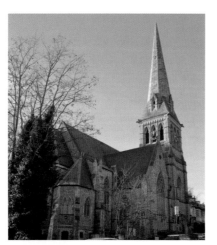

Holy Trinity Church on **Trinity Rise** in Tulse Hill was largely funded by the Cressingham family who laid out what was a wealthy residential district in the 1830s-50s. It was designed by Thomas Denville Barry (1815-1905) to accommodate 1,000 worshippers and was completed in 1856. Grade II listed, it is in the 14th century Decorated style with a broad nave, transepts and a tower surmounted by a stone broach spire which can be seen across Brockwell Park (middle photo: c1910). It is faced with Kentish ragstone with Corsham Down Bath stone dressings. Top left photo: c1891.

Christ Church on **Union Grove** in Clapham is another Benjamin Ferrey design. Completed in 1862, it has a nave and aisles of almost equal height, all in coursed rubble masonry with freestone dressings, also in the early 14th century style (photo below: c1910). Some of the interior fittings by G.E. Street survive as does his adjacent Domestic Revival-style vicarage of 1865. Both are Grade II listed.

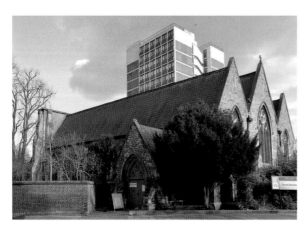

St Peter's Church on **Kennington Lane** is an outstanding Grade II* listed example of mid-Victorian ecclesiastical architecture. It was consecrated in 1864 and was designed by John Pearson (1817-97, architect of Truro Cathedral and the twin towers of Bristol Cathedral) in a 13th century Gothic style. The elevations are of brickwork with stone dressings and it has a slate roof. The intended tower was never built. The interior is magnificent - designed in the Early English style, it is built of yellow stock brick and has ribbed vaulted roofs to the nave, aisles, chancel and chapel. The chancel has an apsidal end with a lancet-windowed clerestory above (the hand-coloured photo above is of c1905).

The **chapel to St Saviour's Almshouses** on **Hamilton Road**, West Norwood is all that survives of this almshouse complex following its rebuilding in 1937 and 1952 (see *Lambeth Architecture 1945-65*) and then the redevelopment of the site creating **Tannoy Square** in 2009. The almshouses moved to Norwood from the parish of St Saviour in north Southwark in 1863 to make way for the Charing Cross Railway Company's new line through Bankside and Waterloo. The chapel, flanked by almshouses, was designed by Edward Habershon and has traceried windows at each end, buttressed walls and a belfry topped by an attenuated fléche. Top photos: 2016 and c1968.

St Leonard's Streatham stands at the junction of **Streatham High Road**, Mitcham Lane and Tooting Bec Road. There has been a church on this site since Norman times or earlier. The church we see today dates back to the 14th century - the tower surviving from this period, with a spire added in 1778. The nave was rebuilt in 1831, six years before Queen Victoria ascended the throne, but the chancel is a notable mid-Victorian addition of 1863. It is of stone with a steep slate roof and was designed in the Early English Gothic style by the artist and a churchwarden of the parish, William Dyce (1806-64) working with the architect Benjamin Ferrey. The vestries were added in 1877. The church was gutted by fire in 1975 but well restored by the Douglas Feast Partnership in 1977. The arcade of columns with stiff-leaf capitals survived the fire. The church is Grade II listed.

Stockwell Baptist Church, 276 South Lambeth Road is an imposing Grade II listed building which has a grand stuccoed pedimented portico with Corinthian columns and flanking bays pilastered at the corners. It was funded by the Lambeth pottery manufacturer James Stiff and opened in 1866. It is pictured above in 1866 and 2016.

St Andrew's Church, Landor Road in Stockwell Green (photo left and a c1910 view on page 9) was built in 1767 as a chapel, extended to the west in 1810 and the exterior was remodelled by Henry Edward Coe in 1867. Coe built the campanile with a pyramidal spire and galleries to the north and south - the galleries were removed in 1924. He added Lombardic-style stucco ornamentation to the Georgian elevations, inserting a large rose window to the eastern front. The church was further extended in 1891 and 1894 when the vestries and Lady Chapel were built by the architect A. J. Pilkington. A roughcast render was applied to the exterior in c1885. It is locally listed.

OLD NORWOOD – Gipsy Hill c1910
(Photograph by Symes)

COLLECTORCARD
Croydon CR0 1HW

C1389

Christ Church, Gipsy Hill was designed by John Giles and consecrated in 1867. The 125 foot (38 metre) Grade II listed tower remains a major landmark but the rest of the church was lost in a fire in 1982. It was a large Kentish ragstone building with Bath stone dressings and slated roofs. It was designed in the French 13th century Gothic manner with polished granite pillars and foliated capitals. It had an apsidal chancel (a semi-circular termination) and a six bay nave with lean-to aisles. The three-stage tower was added in 1889, it had a short octagonal spire and has angled turrets. It was converted into a house named **Highland Tower** in 1998 incorporating a lift and a sympathetic four-storey battlemented side extension faced with render. A new church was built adjacent in 1987 (see *Lambeth Architecture 1965-99*). The top left photo is of c1912 and the bottom image dates from c1903.

The former Anglican **Church of St Jude** on **Dulwich Road** in Herne Hill was begun in 1867 and completed in 1868. The architect was Eric Cookworthy Robins who was selected following a competition for which 12 designs were submitted. The church seated over 1,000 worshippers and is an attractive Victorian Gothic design with a nave of five bays flanked by

aisles. It has a two-stage tower and an ashlar faced spire. The elevations are of Kentish ragstone in the English Decorated style with buttresses, the windows have Geometrical tracery. The church was severely damaged by fire in 1923 and was restored by George Fellowes Prynne. The church closed in the 1975 and it is now business premises. The two engravings date from c1868.

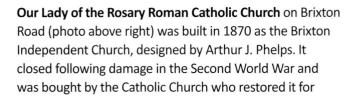

Our Lady of the Rosary Roman Catholic Church on Brixton Road (photo above right) was built in 1870 as the Brixton Independent Church, designed by Arthur J. Phelps. It closed following damage in the Second World War and was bought by the Catholic Church who restored it for their use, reopening in 1953. It is in the Early English Gothic style, built of red brick interspersed with vitrified bricks which give a striped appearance, and has stone dressings. The three-stage tower has a crown of battlements which replaced the original solid brick chisel spire.

The former **Church of St. James the Apostle, Knatchbull Road** overlooks Myatt's Fields Park. The entire cost of the building was met by the landowner James Minet who was laying out the residential neighbourhood at the time. It was designed by George Low to seat 780 people and built in 1870, designed in the Decorated Gothic style, and is built of Kentish

ragstone and Bath stone dressings. It has a clerestoried nave flanked by lean-to aisles terminating in short gabled transepts. The almost free-standing tower has octagonal

corner buttresses and canopied pinnacles below a graceful steeple. Grade II listed in 1979, it was declared redundant in 1981 and converted to flats (Black Roof House). Top photos: 2016 and c1870.

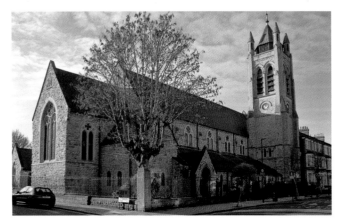

The **former Church of St Saviour** on **Lambert Road** in Brixton was designed by E.C. Robins in the French 13th century style. Seating 900 worshippers it was completed in 1875. Grade II listed, it is built of Kentish ragstone with Bath stone dressings. It has a nave with six arcaded bays, aisles with lean-to roofs, a short lower chancel and a square pinnacled tower with angle buttresses and an octagonal louvered lantern topped by a conical spire. It ceased to be an Anglican church in 1976, becoming a **New Testament Church of God**. Photo above: 1980.

St John the Divine, Vassall Road in North Brixton is one of the finest churches in South London, acknowledged by its Grade I listing. It is also arguably the best work of its renowned architect George Edmund Street (1824-81). It was built in 1874, the tower being added in 1889. It is of the Decorated Gothic style - red brick with stone dressings on the parapets, the surrounds to the traceried windows and the doorways. The tall west tower is a local landmark. It has a broach spire with lucarnes (dormer windows) at three levels. The broad nave has narrow side aisles with tall arcades and is served by a chancel with an apsidal end on the south elevation. The interior was decorated by George Bodley in 1892. The church was hit by an oil bomb in 1940 and then a fire bomb in 1941, destroying its lavish interior however it was restored by H.S. Goodhart Rendel 1958. Photo above right: c1910.

The Grade II* listed **St Paul's Church** on **Rectory Grove**, Clapham (top photo) is a late-Georgian classical-style edifice by Christopher Edmonds built in 1815 but it has a substantial east end addition by Sir Arthur Blomfield erected in 1875. Blomfield was a son of a Bishop of London and uncle to the renowned architect Sir Reginald Blomfield. Arthur also designed the Royal College of Music on Marylebone Road (1882), the nave of Southwark Cathedral (1897) and dozens of parish churches throughout the country. At St Paul's he

chose the very different Romanesque style for the extension albeit employing the same stock facing brick as the original church. The addition comprised a chancel, north and south transepts with open pediments together with an apsidal sanctuary. It was partitioned off from the original church in 1970 to create a church hall.

St Anne's Church (bottom right) stands on the corner of **South Lambeth Road** and Miles Street. Originally built in 1793 as a 'Chapel of Ease' (seen in this watercolour of 1830), it was badly damaged by a fire in 1856 and was reconstructed by R. Parkinson in 1876. It is a Romanesque design - stock brick diapered with red brick and stone dressings, and has a modest tower with a shallow pyramidal roof.

South Lambeth Chapel.

Christ Church — Kennington

The Lincoln Tower (named after the American president) on the corner of **Westminster Bridge Road** and Kennington Road is all that remains of **Christ Church and Upton Chapel** and the attached Hawkstone Hall (photos above: 1931 and left: c1910). Designed in the Early English style by H.J. Paull and Alfred Bickerdike and built in 1876, the church had an octagonal plan. The buildings were damaged in an air raid in 1940, demolished in c1958 and replaced by an office block and a new church (see *Lambeth Architecture 1945-65*). The Grade II listed Kentish ragstone tower has Bath stone dressings; the spire has red stone bands alternating with rows of stars representing the American flag.

Streatham Baptist Church, 22 Lewin Road (top photo) was erected in 1877 on land given by a local farmer, Caleb Higgs. It was extended in 1902 when the imposing tower was added at the east end. It has an octagonal spire with stone pinnacles and gargoyles on the corners. The nave is aligned broadside to the street with a wide transept terminating in a red brick gabled street frontage richly decorated with yellow brick buttresses, arches and banding. The new entrance hall was built in c1994. The church is locally listed.

The former **Trinity Presbyterian Church** (Trinity United Reform Church from 1972) and now the **New Covenant Church, 27-29 Pendennis Road** in Streatham was designed by the well known architects Sir Ernest George and Harold Peto who designed many fine townhouses in Kensington and Chelsea, and country houses in the Home Counties and elsewhere. This Grade II listed church was completed in 1877 in the vernacular revival-style. It is of stock brick with red brick and stone dressings - the west front has a large window with cinquefoil and sexfoil lights (circular windows with five and six petals radiating from the centre) above lancets. The intended tall tower over the entrance was never built. The nave has a scissor-braced roof. This is Ernest George's only surviving unaltered church following the demolition of St Andrews, Guildersfield Road (see entry on page 179). Photos above: c1912 and 2016, the exterior little changed except for the loss of the ivy.

The **former school room**, later the church hall, to the **Streatham Hill Congregational Church, 235 Brixton Hill** (demolished in 1982 - see entry on page 172) was designed by Rowland Plumbe (1838-1919) and built in 1878. It has a T-plan with elevations of stock brick with red brick bands and dressings (top photo). The double-height hall has a magnificent timber roof with king posts and hammerbeams. Now **3-8 Rush Common Mews**, it was saved from demolition by a Grade II spot-listing in 1997 and converted into flats with imaginative contemporary townhouses added at each end.

The former **St Paul's** (now **Brixton Seventh Day Adventist**) on **Santley Street** was designed by William Gilbee Habershon (see also page 173) and E. Fawckner (middle view) and consecrated by the Bishop of Rochester in 1881. It is of yellow brick with courses of red brick and has a hammerbeam roof. The tower planned for the west end was never built. In 1980 the congregation 'swapped' premises with the smaller Adventist Church on Ferndale Road. Three years later and three streets to the west is another Decorated Gothic-style church - the Grade II listed **Brixton (Kenyon) Baptist Chapel** on **Solon Road** (bottom photos of 2016 and c1910). It was built in 1884 in memory of the noted local builder William

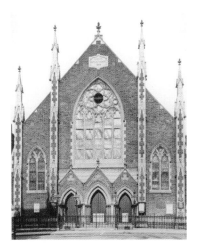

Higgs (1825-83) by his family. It has two façades - the elaborate Decorated Gothic west front of coursed brown sandstone with pale yellow terracotta dressings (made by J. Stiff & Sons, Lambeth), sadly shorn of its pinnacles, has a central triple entrance and large five-light window; and a plainer east front with a rose window.

St Peter's Church on **Clapham Manor Street** and Prescott Place has gable ended frontages with wheel and lancet windows on both streets (the east front is pictured top left, the interior top right). The tall nave has side aisles and an aisled chancel. A bellcote stands above the crossing. It was designed by J.E.K. Cutts (1847-1938), built in 1884 and is Grade II listed. The nave has a polychromatic interior, timber roof and wrought iron screens by W. Bainbridge Reynolds. Charles Eamer Kempe designed the stained glass. The attached church hall was added in 1907.

The **Wesleyan Mission Hall, 59 Lyham Road** is now the **King's Acre Methodist Church** (middle photo). Built in 1886 it has a gabled street façade decorated with carved brick and pargetting (decorated render). It has a tall Venetian window and a lower side extension.

The former **People's Church** on **Grafton Square** in Clapham (now flats) could be mistaken for a late Victorian town hall (bottom photo). It was designed by William Nevin and built in 1889. Two short towers flank an elegant colonnaded porch.

Corpus Christi Roman Catholic Church stands at the junction of **Brixton Hill** and Trent Road (top photos - the interior view was taken in c1950) and is an outstanding example of the Early Decorated Gothic 14th century style. It was designed by one of the most talented church architects of the Victorian period, J.F. Bentley (1839-1902), and built in stages between 1886 and 1904. Only the Chancel and transepts were ever completed. The nave, tower, a side chapel, a presbytery and the north and south aisles were never built. The elevations are of striped red brick and Bath stone. It is listed Grade II*.

The **former St Matthew's Church Hall** (now **St Vincent's Community Centre**) on the corner of **Talma Road** and Probert Road in Brixton was built in 1889 (middle photo). The locally listed building was designed in an informal picturesque style with an octagonal tower on the corner. The elevations are of stock brick with red brick quoins, window headers and aprons, buttresses dividing the bays.

The locally listed **Gresham Baptist Chapel** in East Brixton has handsome classical brick and stucco façades with pediments to the central bays on both **Barrington Road** and **Gresham Road** (bottom photo). It opened in 1880 but after a fire it was rebuilt in 1897 when the foundation stone was unveiled by the publisher Horace Brooks Marshall who became Lord Mayor of London in 1918 and Baron Marshall of Chipstead in 1922.

St. Peter's Church on **Leigham Court Road** in Streatham is an outstanding Grade II* listed church. The eastern end comprising the chancel, vestries and three bays of the nave, was designed by Richard Drew and built in 1871. The church was completed in 1887 by George Fellowes Prynne (1853-1927, a prolific church architect whose works include All Saints, West Dulwich and Christ Church Cathedral in Colombo in Ceylon, now Sri Lanka) who added two bays to the nave together with an octagonal baptistery. It is a Decorated Gothic-style building in yellow brick banded and diapered in red brick with Bath stone dressings.

The West Front is particularly impressive (seen in the recent top view and the bottom left photo of 1892). The tall gable to the nave has a large wheel window flanked by octagonal turrets, rising above the baptistery which is lit by a triple arcade of lancet windows. The interior has stone columns supporting wide pointed arches below the wooden roof resting on arch-braced collar beams and scissor trusses. The Lady Chapel has a three sided apse and is entered through a wrought-iron screen.

The Grade I listed **All Saints' Church** on **Lovelace Road** and Rosendale Road in West Dulwich was designed by Fellowes Prynne at the same time as he was supervising the construction of St Peter's, Streatham. The foundation stone was laid by the Bishop of Rochester in 1888, and the completed portion of the building was opened in 1891. The entire cost of the church was met by the local residents of this affluent district. It has a commanding presence visible for miles around but only four of the intended seven bays of the nave were built and the tower at the west end seen in the bottom image of 1893 was never completed. It has been described as 'eclectic Gothic' in style and possibly inspired by Erfurt Cathedral in Germany. The elevations are of a warm red brick with stone dressings. The east front is dominated by the chancel apse and its five elongated three-light windows.

It was damaged in 1944 during the Second World War but repaired in 1952 when a belfry designed by John Comper was erected in memory of the parishioners killed in the war. In 2000 a fire gutted the church but it was repaired and remodelled in 2006. The reconstructed interior is quite breathtaking - it has a wagon vault roof above the semi-circular moulded brick arches that form the nave arcades.

The **Roman Catholic Church of the English Martyrs** is a beautiful landmark at the junction of **Mitcham Lane** and Streatham High Road. Grade II* listed, it was designed in the French Gothic style by Alfred Edward Purdie (1843-1920), a pupil of Augustus Pugin, and built in 1892. It has a broach spire, walls of Kentish ragstone with Bath stone dressings and traceried windows (top photos: 2016 and 1903).

The former **St Matthias Church** at **41 Upper Tulse Hill** (bottom photos: c1910 and 2016) is built of red brick with a steep tiled roof and lancet windows. Built in 1894, it has been a Gospel Tabernacle since 1981.

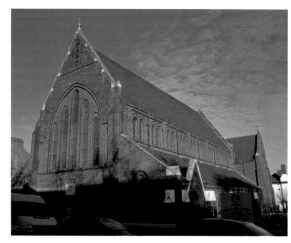

St Andrew's Church on **Guildersfield Road** in Streatham was lost in 1991 (see page 179) but its **church hall** (top and middle photos) survives in a new use - the Streatham Common Practice doctors' surgery. The hall was completed in 1898, designed by Sir Ernest George (1839-1922) working with Alfred Yeates, who built the church and the still extant (Grade II listed) vicarage in 1886. George also designed Southwark Bridge, houses on the Cadogan estate in Chelsea and several country houses. The Grade II listed vernacular revival-style hall is built of brick with a tiled roof. The semi-circular porch hood has the name in Arts and Crafts lettering.

The Grade II listed former **Christ Church Hall** on **Mowll Street** sits behind the church of 1907 on Brixton Road. Both were designed by Arthur Beresford Pite (1861-1934). The hall was built in 1898 and used for worship until the church was finished. It has a dramatic façade dominated by a giant Diocletian window which incorporates the pair of entrance doors. The composition is crowned by an open bellcote. Bottom photos: 2016 and 1968.

Streatham Methodist Church stands on the corner of **Mitcham Lane** and Riggindale Road and was built in 1900 to a design by Wheeler & Speed (top photos: 2016 and c1912). It is a good example of a fusion of the Art Nouveau and Gothic styles with red brick elevations decorated with stone. Generous windows with segmental, square-headed or Tudor arched lintels light the interior. **Streatham United Reformed Church, 388 Streatham High Road** was completed in 1901 by James Cubitt. It has a noble battlemented tower and is built of red brick with stone dressings (bottom photos: 2016 and c1905). Both churches are Grade II listed.

The former **St. Cuthbert's English Presbyterian Church** occupies an elevated site on the South Circular (**Thurlow Park Road**) in Tulse Hill (top photos: 2016 and 1925). Locally listed, it was designed by Arthur Owen Breeds combining Arts and Crafts and Gothic influences. Built in 1901, it is built of red brick with stone dressings and has a tower surmounted by a copper spire. It became a United Reform Church in 1972 but closed in 1990 and it is now part of Rosemead School.

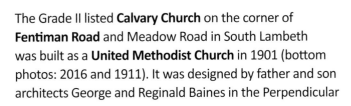

The Grade II listed **Calvary Church** on the corner of **Fentiman Road** and Meadow Road in South Lambeth was built as a **United Methodist Church** in 1901 (bottom photos: 2016 and 1911). It was designed by father and son architects George and Reginald Baines in the Perpendicular style with elevations of red brick and stone dressings. The commanding tower has crenellated battlements with gargoyles and traceried windows. Attached to the north west is a former Sunday School which has an arch-braced roof and stained glass depicting tulips and lilies.

West Norwood Cemetery on **Norwood Road** is one of the so-called "Magnificent Seven" private cemeteries established in London between 1832 and 1841 to alleviate overcrowding in the city's existing burial grounds, the others being Kensal Green, Highgate, Abney Park, Nunhead, Brompton and Tower Hamlets. Also known as the South Metropolitan Cemetery, the 40 acre site is entered through a Gothic gateway (seen bottom right in c1890). It has one of the finest collections of monuments, tombs and mausoleums in London, over 65 of which are listed. When it was opened by the Bishop of Winchester in 1837, the area was still largely rural as can be seen in the top image of 1853, which shows its careful planning and picturesque landscaping by its designer Sir William Tite. A Church of England chapel was built on the summit and another chapel was built for the Nonconformists, both were demolished in the 1950s. A plethora of well-known Victorians are buried here including Mrs Beeton, Sir Henry Tate, Baron von Reuter, Sir Henry Bessemer and architects William Burges and Sir William Tite. The tombs pictured here are of Alexander Berens (c1858) and Eustratios Rali (c1875), both designed by E.M. Barry. Middle view: c1891.

An acre was set aside as a burial ground for the Greek community in 1842. It has a fine classical chapel by John Oldrid Scott (Grade II* listed - top photo).

Pictured below left is the mausoleum of Sir Henry Doulton (1820-97), the Lambeth pottery magnate, made of red brick and terracotta, the entrance decorated with reliefs of angels in the spandrels. Below is a sketch of the cemetery on the front cover of a guide published in 1857.

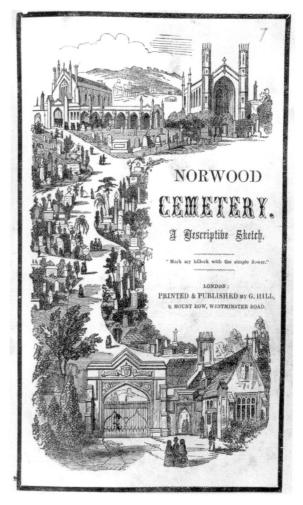

LOST LAMBETH

The roll-call of lost Victorian buildings in Lambeth is grievous to relate. A good many were destroyed or badly damaged during the bombing raids of the Second World War. Others survived the war but were deemed uneconomic due to changing public policy, such as the closure of large welfare, health or educational institutions. Other buildings, particularly places of worship or entertainment were too large or too numerous for modern-day needs. Another key factor was that Victorian architecture was widely considered to be old fashioned and expendable in the 1950s and 1960s, a view that only began to change in the 1970s as the conservation movement gained strength and they became far more appreciated.

The first part of this chapter records churches that are now no more - most were demolished in the 1950s and 60s, but some as recently as the 1980s. Pictured here is **Holy Trinity Church** on **Carlisle Lane**, north east of Archbishop's Park. Built in 1839 in the Romanesque architectural style in Suffolk grey brick with a modest tower, it was constructed on land that was part of Lambeth Palace's kitchen garden. The church, which seated 800 worshippers, was designed by Edward Blore (1787-1879) who had recently undertaken the major remodelling and extension of Lambeth Palace itself. The church was restored in 1915 by Charles Nicholson when a large conspicuous red cross was erected on the east wall visible to passengers on trains entering Waterloo. It sustained severe damage in the Blitz and stood in ruins for many years (seen

in the top photo in c1954 when it was a roofless shell) until its demolition in 1956 (photo bottom right). Today it is a car park (bottom left).

ALL SAINTS CHURCH, LAMBETH.

All Saints, Lower Marsh was built in 1846 on a site now occupied by Station Approach, the cab road serving Waterloo Station, and the railway lines leading into platforms 1 and 2 (see photo below). It was built on Duchy of Cornwall land two years before Waterloo Station opened in 1848. Designed by architect William Rogers (architect of St Michael's, Stockwell Park - see entry on page 142) in the Anglo-Norman style, it had a 160 foot (nearly 50 metres) spire, seen in the top engraving of 1846 from the Illustrated London News, and seated 1,500 worshippers. The tower suffered from subsidence and was removed later in the century,

followed by the rest of the church in 1901 to make way for the enlargement of Waterloo Station. The parish was then united with St John the Evangelist, Waterloo.

All Saints, Clapham Park on **Lyham Road** in Brixton Hill was built in 1858 (bottom left photo: c1905) and was a most impressive composition with its tall steeple and Kentish ragstone tower and nave. It was designed by Thomas Talbot Bury (1809-77) who worked with Pugin and Barry on the

designs for the Houses of Parliament in the 1830s. Sadly by 1980 it had become structurally unsound and was demolished in 1982, to be replaced by a much more modest building built of yellow brick with an echo of the original steeple (see photo left and entry in *Lambeth Architecture 1965-99*).

Streatham Hill Congregational Church stood on **Brixton Hill** opposite Morrish Road from c1860 until it was pulled down in 1982 and replaced by a new place of worship (photo below right). Its slender stone spire pictured top left in c1905 was a major landmark and its beautiful

interior included a monumental organ seen in this view from c1932. Its demolition was a great loss. The church hall of 1878 to the rear survives as flats (see entry on page 159).

The original **Church of St Stephen** on **St Stephen's Terrace**, just off Albert Square was a large mid-Victorian Decorated Gothic design faced with Kentish ragstone with Bath stone dressings (bottom left photo: 1967). The steeple was flanked with octagonal pinnacles with dormers to the

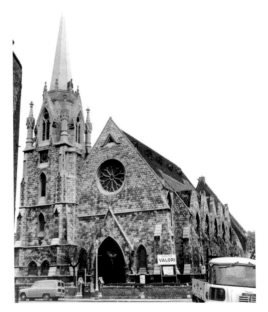

belfry. Built in 1861 by architect John Barnett, it could seat 1,200 worshippers. By the mid-1960s attendance had declined to a fifth of that number and the decision was taken to demolish and replace it with a much smaller church (photo left) and flats built in 1967-69.

St Philip's Church stood at the corner of **Kennington Road** and Reedworth Street (bottom right photo: c1905). It was begun in 1849 and consecrated in 1863, seating 600 worshippers. Bombed twice in the Second World War, it was repaired but then declared redundant in 1975 and demolished in 1976. The site is now Archbishop Sumner School garden (top right view).

Loughborough Park Congregational Chapel stood on the corner of **Coldharbour Lane** and Herne Hill Road (engraving below). Built in 1860, it was designed by W.G. Habershon (1818-91) in a Lombardic style with tall lancet windows and a large wheel window above the entrance porch on the north front. A Sunday School at the rear was added in 1862 and a tower in c1880. The church closed in 1941, when the congregation transferred to Herne Hill United Reform Church. It served as a warehouse until it was razed in c1962 and redeveloped (pictured bottom left).

St Philip's Church, Lambeth.

St. Saviour's Church, Herne Hill Road stood in front of St Saviour's Primary School (built in 1869) from its consecration by the Bishop of Winchester in 1867 to its demolition (together with its vicarage, no. 67) in 1981. It was designed in a Romanesque style by A.D. Gough (1804-71), the chancel and south transepts were added later by W. Gibbs Bartleet. The ragstone elevations were dressed with Bath stone; the five-stage tower had an arcaded top section beneath a pyramidal roof (top photo: c1975). The aisled nave had four bays and seated 850 worshippers. The church was declared redundant in 1973 when it was relocated to the nearby church hall of 1915 designed by Beresford Pite (see *Lambeth's Edwardian Splendours*). The site of the church was used as an extension to the playground and a new classroom block (middle left photo).

St Saviour's Church, Clapham on **Cedars Road** was designed by the prolific J.T. Knowles and completed in 1864 (pictured below in 1900). It was built in the Decorated Gothic style with a central tower topped by pinnacles. The stained glass was by Clayton and Bell. It was destroyed by a bomb in 1940 and the site was sold in 1962 to the LCC to form part of its Cedars Road Estate - photo bottom left - the same site today.

Trinity Presbyterian Church stood on **Clapham Road**, opposite Clitheroe Road from 1862 until its demolition in c1957. It had a noble Bath stone portico of Roman Corinthian columns crowned by a giant pediment, the side elevations were of stock brick with tall arched windows. It

is pictured far left in 1900, the photo left is its mundane replacement, a printing works built in 1959, now a tool hire depot.

The **Mostyn Road Methodist Church** in North Brixton was a more recent loss. Designed by John Tarring & Sons, the foundation stone was laid in 1868. It was faced with Kentish ragstone. The bottom left photo taken in 1906 shows its soaring steeple at the junction of Lawrence Road (now Lawrence Way) with a turret at the far end, which was the Sunday School. Although the church sustained war damage, it was repaired in 1954-55, only to be torn down in c1982. In 1987 it was replaced by a smaller red brick church (photo below) and a block of flats.

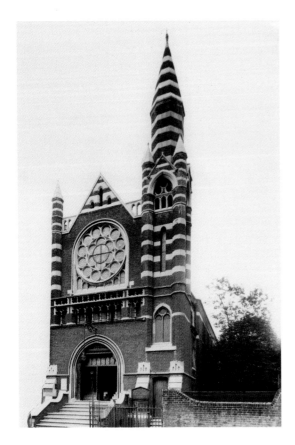

Wynne Road Baptist Church, just off Brixton Road, was an extraordinary Free Gothic-style chapel built in 1877 (top photos: 1938). It had a tower and spire in banded brick and stone, a giant

rose window, a lofty interior with galleries and a great hammer beam roof. It was destroyed during the Blitz, the site was redeveloped as the Nona Works in the 1940s and then again for a nursing home in 1995 (photo left).

St James' Church on **Park Hill** in Clapham by Cachemaille-Day built in 1958 is the finest post-war church in Lambeth (photo left) but its predecessor, destroyed by a bomb in 1940, was also of great interest. It was built in 1829 by Lewis Vulliamy and greatly enlarged in 1871 by F.J. and H. Francis who added the pinnacled tower, chancel and transepts seen in the far left photo taken in 1898.

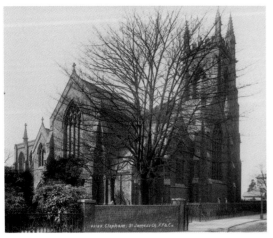

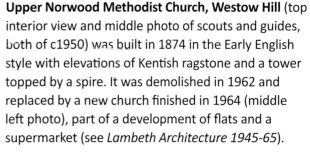

Upper Norwood Methodist Church, Westow Hill (top interior view and middle photo of scouts and guides, both of c1950) was built in 1874 in the Early English style with elevations of Kentish ragstone and a tower topped by a spire. It was demolished in 1962 and replaced by a new church finished in 1964 (middle left photo), part of a development of flats and a supermarket (see *Lambeth Architecture 1945-65*).

Chatsworth Baptist Church on **Chatsworth Way** in West Norwood was built in 1877 (bottom left photo: c1925). In 1900 two large halls and a lecture room were added behind. In September 1944 the first V2 rocket to land on Lambeth made a direct

hit on the church (photo left: the day after the bomb) destroying everything within the strong outer walls. Bibles and hymn books were found as far as Streatham. The remains of the church were cleared and in 1959 a new church by Arthur Bailey was built, seen in the bottom right photo (see entry in *Lambeth Architecture 1945-65*).

St Agnes on **St Agnes Place**, Kennington Park was a very large and handsome church with a capacity of 1,200 worshippers and a strong Anglo-Catholic tradition. It was designed by George Gilbert Scott Junior (1839-1897) in 1874, consecrated in 1877 by the Bishop of London, but not completed until 1890 (the exterior views are of 1888 and 1920, the latter with Scott's vicarage in the foreground). It was of red brick from Suffolk and Hampshire with Bath stone dressings designed in the 14th century Decorated neo-Gothic style. The nave was unusually tall and magnificently decorated (see top photo: Christmas 1901). It possessed outstanding stained glass by Charles Eamer Kempe (1837-1907) and lavish interior fittings by Temple Moore (1856-1920, a pupil of Scott). The church suffered heavy war damage in 1941 when it lost its roof (though the furnishings were salvaged) but could have been repaired. Despite a

campaign by the likes of John Betjeman (later the Poet Laureate) and Stephen Dykes Bower to save it, the church was demolished and replaced by a new design in 1956 by Ralph Covell (see *Lambeth Architecture 1945-65*, and the bottom right photo).

The site of the Co-op supermarket and flats on **Norwood Road** opposite Tulse Hill station approach was previously occupied by the very fine **Roupell Park Methodist Church** (top left photo: 1910). The architect of this Early English-style landmark was Charles Bell (1844-99) who designed a number of Methodist churches throughout London including the imposing Bermondsey Central Hall and South London Mission of 1900. The foundation stone was laid in June 1879 and the building was completed the following year. It was set back from Norwood Road behind railings and gate piers topped with lanterns. The church was faced with Kentish ragstone with Bath stone dressings and on its north-east corner stood a tower with a clock (added later in 1888) above which soared a

stone spire. A vast gable end faced east and to the west was an apsidal end. It was demolished in 1967 to be replaced by the supermarket, flats and a much smaller church to the rear of the site, designed by Shepherd, Fowler & Marshall (photo left).

St Andrew's Church on **Guildersfield Road** in Streatham was a tragic loss (bottom left photo: c1912). It was designed by George & Peto and built in 1889. It was Grade II listed in 1981 but declared redundant in 1988, and demolished after a fire in 1992. Housing now occupies the site (below).

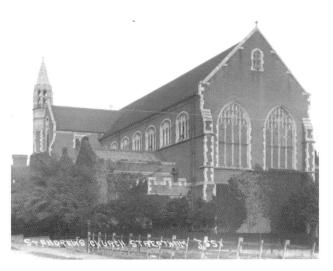

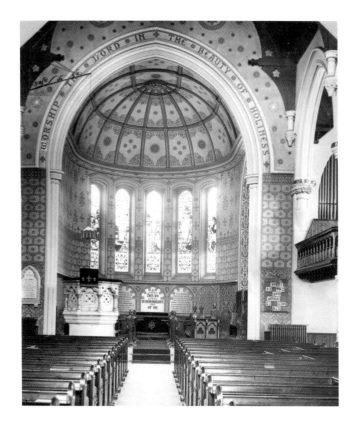

STREATHAM, FROM THE AIR. WESLEYAN, ST. LEONARD'S AND R.C. CHURCHES. No. 1046

Streatham Methodist Church stood on the corner of **Streatham High Road** and Stanthorpe Road. Designed by Charles Bell and built in 1882, it was an imposing building with an elegant spire and a spectacular interior (top photos: c1932 and c1905, aerial view: c1924). It was demolished in 1967 and replaced by a block of shops and flats (photo left) designed by David Stern and Partners.

The **Lion Brewery** stood on the **South Bank** from 1837 until its demolition in 1949 to make way for the Royal Festival Hall (middle photo) and part of the Festival of Britain site (see *Lambeth Architecture 1945-65*). Designed by architect Francis Edwards (1784-1857), it was an imposing five-storey classical riverside building with Roman Doric columns standing on a rusticated stone ground-floor and a giant lion made of Coade stone (a ceramic material perfected by Eleanor Coade in c1770) standing proudly above the façade (top right photo: c1920). A second smaller lion stood above the entrance screen on **Belvedere Road** (top left photo: c1885).

The brewery closed after a major fire in 1931. The large lion was salvaged before the demolition at the request of King George VI. It was relocated first to Waterloo Station Approach in 1951 and then to a plinth beside County Hall and Westminster Bridge in 1966 where it still stands today (bottom photo). The second, smaller lion was eventually re-erected in 1971 to stand outside the Twickenham Rugby stadium where it was covered in gold leaf in 1991.

HUNGERFORD AND LAMBETH SUSPENSION BRIDGE.

The **Hungerford and Lambeth Suspension Footbridge** was opened in 1845 linking the South Bank with the Hungerford Market hall built between the Strand and the river in 1833. The bridge was designed by Sir Isambard Kingdom Brunel and comprised two lofty Italianate towers rising above piers, which carried the heavy chains (top engraving from *The Builder* published in 1845). The 676 foot central span was the largest in Britain at the time. After only 15 years in use it was rebuilt as a railway bridge to serve the new Charing Cross station in 1860-64 (see p. 69) built on the site of the market.

The **Canterbury Music Hall** had a tall entrance block at **143 Westminster Bridge Road** (seen in the left print of c1885, bottom left lithograph of 1858 and 1893 programme below) linked via a tunnel under the railway viaduct to the huge auditorium block on the other side. It opened in 1852 and was rebuilt several times in 1856, 1876 and then in 1890 by the renowned theatre architect, Frank Matcham (1854-1920). The theatre had a sliding roof for ventilation. It became a very popular venue for variety, ballet, light music and comedy, and was patronized by royalty.

It became a cinema in the 1920s but was destroyed by a wartime bomb in 1942. The site of the auditorium lies buried beneath the railway viaduct built in 1990-93 for the Eurostar terminal at Waterloo. The site of the entrance block is now a storage yard.

THE CANTERBURY.

The original **Brixton Police Station** (top photo: c1910), **367 Brixton Road** was erected at the junction of Gresham Road in 1858 to the design of Charles Reeves, Metropolitan Police Surveyor. The Survey of London in 1956 described the design as having 'a distinct flavour of Vanbrugh' and it was similar to Reeves's slightly earlier Gipsy Hill Police Station which survives as flats today (see entry on page 14). It was replaced on the same site by a larger police station in 1959 seen in the middle left photo (see *Lambeth Architecture 1945-65*).

In 1852 the Earl of Lonsdale laid the foundation stone for the **Westmorland Society School** at **44-52 Norwood Road** in Tulse Hill. It was a grandiose Jacobean-style building with moulded Dutch-style gables designed by George Smith (bottom left photo: c1894). It closed in the 1920s, becoming the Westmorland Garage. The former school building was demolished in 1964 (photo left) and the site is now occupied by flats (middle right photo).

Although Lambeth was spared the Beeching cuts that decimated the nation's railway system in the 1960s and resulted in the loss of many very fine Victorian station buildings, it did lose one in 1976 when **East Brixton station** closed. Opened in 1866, it had two timber platforms with weather-boarded buildings overhanging each side of the viaduct, supported on cast iron columns and lattice girders (photos - top left: 1975, middle: 1964 and top right: 2016). Stairs led down to entrances on **Barrington Road**.

West Norwood station (bottom photos of c1935 and 2015) on **Knight's Hill** lost its charming timber station buildings of 1859 (similar to Streatham Hill's, see entry on page 66) in the early 1970s, replaced by a prefabricated design.

The **Norwood Institute** on the corner of **Knight's Hill** and Chapel Road was built in 1858. The original three-storey ragstone-faced building with a short battlemented tower is pictured in the engraving below of c1880 and the top left photo of c1920. It was founded by Arthur Anderson *'to promote the moral, intellectual and social improvement of the Inhabitants residing within a radius of five miles'*, teaching such subjects as domestic science and commerce. It was extended in the 1900s and acquired by the LCC in 1904. In 1948 the name was changed to **Norwood Technical College** and twenty years later to the **South London College**. In 1969-74 the college was redeveloped with a new building by the Inner London Education Authority. The top right photo shows the most regrettable demolition of the building in 1969. The 1970s buildings were themselves demolished in 2000 following the closure of the college and the vacant site is seen below in 2016.

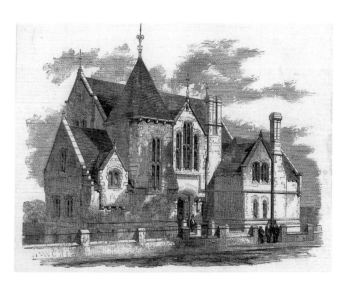

CITY OF LONDON ORPHAN SCHOOL, BRIXTON.—Mr. Bunning, Architect.

In 1854 the City of London opened its **Freemen's Orphan School** on **Ferndale Road** with a roll of 100 children. It was designed by the Corporation's architect, James Bunstone Bunning - the imposing classical façade is seen in the engraving of 1854 (top). The middle photo is of the interior of the main hall in c1905. It was enlarged in 1863 but the school relocated to Ashtead Park in Surrey in 1924. The building was demolished and replaced by Ferndale Court, City of London Police flats, designed by Sydney Perks and built in 1929. It was renamed St Edmundsbury Court after acquisition by Lambeth Housing department in the 1970s.

The British and Foreign School Society's **Stockwell Training College** for Schoolmistresses was a commanding six-storey landmark on **Stockwell Road** from its inauguration in 1861 (see bottom left engraving of c1890), designed by William Beck in a grand Italianate style. The college had schools attached for the students to complete their teacher training practice. It was pulled down in the 1930s by the LCC to build Acland House and Blair House on its Stockwell Gardens Estate, completed in 1937 (pictured below).

Norwood Jewish Orphanage, off **Knight's Hill** was opened in 1863, the foundation stone was laid by Sir Anthony de Rothschild. It resembled a large Jacobean mansion (top photo: c1930) - red brick with diaper (criss-cross patterned) black brickwork - a synagogue in the central portion. It housed some 400 children by the 1910s, training the girls for domestic service and the boys in engineering, leatherworking, clothing manufacture and office work. The main building closed in 1961 and was tragically demolished. A much smaller synagogue and community hall was built in its place (see *Lambeth Architecture 1945-65*). Only its lodge survives (see page 41). The site was redeveloped again for the West Norwood Health & Leisure Centre, opened in 2014 (bottom right).

The **Magdalen Hospital** on **Drewstead Road** in Streatham was designed by Henry Currey and built in 1869 as a home for 'penitent prostitutes'. It became an approved school for female offenders in 1934, closing in 1966 to make way for Lambeth Council's Magdalen Estate. Only the lodge survives - it is locally listed. The chapel is pictured below in 1890.

Lambeth Bridge is a handsome 18 metre wide structure designed by Sir Reginald Blomfield, built in 1932 (see *Lambeth Architecture 1914-39* and photo below right) but it was preceded by a very different suspension bridge of 1862 (pictured below in 1866), demolished in 1929.

It was designed by the civil engineer Peter Barlow (brother of William Barlow, the engineer who designed St Pancras station train shed) and was 10m wide. It had such steep approaches and was in such poor condition by 1910 that it was restricted to pedestrian traffic only.

The railways that criss-cross the borough exert a huge influence on Lambeth's development and townscape. Herne Hill in particular is dominated by seven major railway bridges. There are two that cross over **Rosendale Road** (see entries on page 69) but there used to be a third that served the Knight's Hill goods station and coal yards

from the time of its construction by the London & North Western Railway in 1891 until its closure by British Rail in 1967. The depot was then redeveloped as the Lairdale Estate in 1975-80 (see *Lambeth Architecture 1965-99*). The bridge is pictured bottom left in c1966 before its removal and (bottom right) the surviving abutments in 2016.

Gatti's Music Hall was a popular Victorian entertainment venue at **218 Westminster Bridge Road** (top left photo: c1945) which stood between the former Eurostar terminal at Waterloo and the Park Plaza hotel. It hosted many music hall stars including Marie Lloyd, Harry Lauder and Dan Leno. Built in 1865 as a restaurant by the Italian Swiss entrepreneur Carlos Gatti, it was then rebuilt and enlarged as Gatti's Palace of Varieties in 1883 with a capacity of over 1,000. It became the Gatti Picture Palace cinema in 1924

but was damaged during the Second World War. Its fine Italianate-style frontage block survived, only to be demolished by the LCC in 1950 to make way for its new road scheme. The GLC later built its County Hall Island Block in 1974, demolished in 2006 to make way for the Park Plaza hotel - see photo left of the site today.

Hammerton's Brewery stood on the corner of **Stockwell Green** and Lingham Street opposite St Andrew's Church (see page 151) for over a century. Its solid late-Victorian buildings are pictured above in 1964 shortly before it was replaced by a Truman's bottling plant which in turn was removed for the present day Oak Square residential development (photo right).

Pratt's Department Store on **Streatham High Road** was founded by George Pratt in the 1850s. The original premises at **121-127** is seen in the top photo in c1890 - note the elegant plate glass shop windows and fascia of glass and gilded lettering. The buildings still stand today, though sadly their fine shopfronts have been replaced. Pratt's expanded across the road to Eldon House (**210-224**) and served South Londoners for over 130 years. By the 1900s the store offered a wide choice of home furnishings, china and glassware.

In 1920 it was sold to Bon Marche of Brixton and then six years later it was taken over by Selfridges as a branch of their Provincial Stores group. The middle photo dates from this part of its history, shown in 1935 bedecked with flags to celebrate King George V's Silver Jubilee. It was bought in 1940 by the John Lewis Partnership which ran the store until its closure in 1990. The buildings were demolished (see bottom left photo taken in 1995) and redeveloped for a Lidl supermarket and an Argos store which opened in 1996 (below).

The **South Western Hospital** on **Landor Road** in Brixton is now the Lambeth Hospital providing mental health services (photo left), but it was built in 1871 to treat small pox and fevers, such as typhoid, typhus and scarlet fever. Most of the original Victorian buildings (top photos: c1914) were redeveloped in 1996 but Landor House, the lodge and gate piers survive (see p.37).

The original **Lambeth Hospital** was off **Renfrew Road** in Kennington (bottom photo: 1966 and plan) built in 1876 as the **Lambeth Workhouse Infirmary** (see p. 34). The two right hand ward blocks were demolished, one in 1937 to build a new maternity wing and the other in 1966 for a new operating theatre block. The two ward blocks on the left of the plan were demolished in the 1980s after the hospital closed in 1976, replaced by the Woodlands Nursing Home (1995) and housing in 2010.

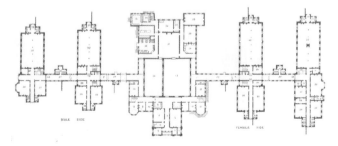

Huge swathes of Victorian housing were demolished in the 1950s, 1960s and 1970s to make way for new local authority estates. Whole neighbourhoods were razed by both the LCC (after 1965, the GLC) and Lambeth Council. These housing programmes are described in detail in the two volumes on *Lambeth Architecture 1945-65* and *1965-99*. Some of the 19th century housing selected for demolition was in a poor state of repair and unfit for habitation, but a significant proportion could have been rehabilitated. Government grants favoured redevelopment and Victorian housing was seen as unfashionable in this period. By the 1970s local residents and conservation groups were sufficiently organised to begin to oppose such schemes and both authorities began to conserve and refurbish older houses as part of their projects. Comprehensive clearances ceased in the early 1980s. Just a few examples of the Victorian housing that was demolished in this period are shown on this and the next page. **Knowle Road** in Brixton is pictured top left in 1908 - tall and spacious four-storey terraced houses most of which survived the Blitz, but were swept away to build the Stockwell Park Estate in the 1970s (middle photo). Most of the modest terraced homes built in the 1870s seen in the aerial view taken in c1950 of the **Milkwood Estate** in Herne Hill were demolished in 1976 to create Milkwood Park (photo below) and a new school.

Pictured here are two Brixton streets 'Then and Now'. **Somerleyton Road** (top left in c1912 and no. 1 in the middle right view in 1962) was demolished to build the Moorlands Estate and Southwyck House (top right) in the 1970s. The middle left photo is of a Victorian terrace built as part of the Angell Town district in c1855 on **St James's Road** (now Crescent) in 1925. It was demolished in the 1950s to build part of the Loughborough Estate seen in the bottom view from the same vantage point 90 years later.

Clapham suffered a sustained destruction of its Victorian heritage in the post-war years as the LCC demolished almost all of Thomas Cubitt's large villas in Clapham Park and J.T. Knowles' grand townhouses on Cedars Road and Victoria Rise, to the north of the Common. Over 50 houses like this one - **3 Cedars Road**

(seen top left in c1930 and below, the site today) were pulled down in the early 1960s to make way for the Cedars Road Estate (see *Lambeth Architecture 1945-65*).

The former **Lambeth Schools** on **Elder Road** in Norwood was founded by the Lambeth Workhouse in 1810 as the **Norwood House of Industry**. It was greatly expanded in

1879-89 when the Italianate buildings in this view (left, photo taken in 1967) were built. The LCC took over the schools in 1930 and closed the institution, converting it to a children's home (renamed Woodvale in 1949), a school, a hostel for the homeless and a rest home (later called Elderwood). The 1850 portion survives in residential use but the later Victorian blocks were demolished in the 1970s to make way for the Woodvale Estate (photo below) leaving only seven gate piers and stretches of railings and front boundary walls as reminders of its former presence.

Lambeth has lost a good many fine pubs, particularly in the last 20 years - just four examples are featured here. **The Windsor Castle, 54 Mayall Road** in Brixton was an elegant pub built in the mid 1870s and stood for over a century on the corner of Leeson Road (top photos below, both taken in c1975). As was the norm in this era, the interior was divided into different bars for the different social classes who preferred to socialise with their own kind, each bar having its own separate entrance, but all served by the same horseshoe-plan bar counter. The

pub survived the bombs of the Second World War but was burnt out by arsonists who threw a petrol bomb into the bar during the Brixton riots in 1981. The 70-year old landlady of the Windsor Castle, Annie Taylor, was nearly burnt alive but was dragged to safety just in time. The site was later cleared, along with the adjoining terrace and replaced by social housing (seen in the middle right photo).

The Queen, 45 Bellefields Road at its junction with Pulross Road, Brixton (pictured bottom left in 1937) was built in the mid-1860s. It had a ground floor prow on the corner and three façades of yellow stock brick framed by stucco quoins. The pub was demolished by developers in 2006 and replaced by a four-storey block of flats given the same name (bottom right view).

The Feathers, 116 Lambeth Walk (top left photo: 1965) had a distinctive façade with curved corner bays and a fan motif on the semi-circular pediment. A pub had stood on this corner of Old Paradise Street since the 18th century but it was rebuilt in the mid-Victorian era. The Feathers

closed in 1965 and was demolished and replaced by a new pub called The George in 1977 as part of the GLC's Lambeth Walk Estate. The site was redeveloped again in 2011 when a new block of flats, Arundel Court, was built (left).

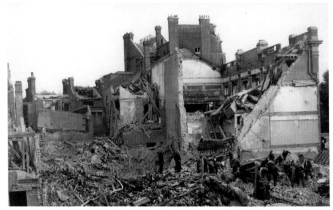

The demolition of the historic **Horns Tavern** and its assembly rooms, on the corner of **Kennington Road** and Kennington Park Road was a sad loss. An inn dating back to the 18th century was rebuilt in 1887 in an opulent late-Victorian style by architects Crickmay and Son (middle left view: c1910). Its attached assembly rooms were destroyed by a V1 rocket in 1944 (photo above right taken from Stannary Street) but the pub was repaired, only to be demolished and replaced by a grim government office block designed by Seifert in 1970 (left).

Wellington Mills on **Westminster Bridge Road**, next to Christ Church, was the home of John Oakey and Sons Ltd from 1874 until they left the site in the 1960s and it was demolished. The site was previously occupied by the Royal Female Orphan Asylum. Oakey and Sons

built a fine Italianate-style factory and four-storey offices designed by Messrs. Parr & Strong, pictured top left in 1933. The offices were lost in the Blitz and rebuilt in a modern classical style in c1948. They were a well known manufacturer of emery cloth, sandpaper, and Wellington Knife Polish. John Oakey is buried in West Norwood Cemetery. The site was redeveloped as the Wellington Mills estate, completed in 1976 (see *Lambeth Architecture 1965-99* and photo below).

Wellington Mills

The **Royal Flour Mills** were established at **90 Albert Embankment** in Vauxhall by Peter Mumford in 1875. Mumford & Sons' other mills were on Deptford Creek including a landmark mill of 1897 designed by Sir Aston Webb (Grade II listed, now flats). The Vauxhall mills comprised a monumental complex of

nine-storey red brick buildings (bottom left photo: c1950). The mills were bought by Charles Brown & Co Ltd in 1927 and closed in c1955. They were demolished to build an office block (Camelford House) in 1960-62 (bottom right photo - see *Lambeth Architecture 1945-65*).

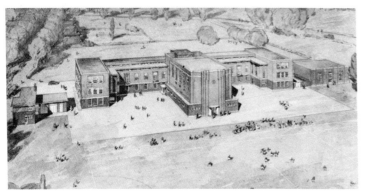

Woodfield on the northern side of **Bedford Hill** in Streatham was a fine residence rebuilt in 1878 by architect Richard Drew. It was a handsome three-storey property in the Old English style with half-timbered and tile-hung gables and a curved conservatory (see top photo: c1905). It was the home of Charles Mortimer JP, a stockbroker in the City and his large household staff. Local historian Graham Gower has ascertained that this included a governess, two grooms, a butler, a footman, a cook, a kitchen maid and nine other servants.

The Mortimer family moved out in 1895, and it became a nursing home until it was demolished in 1935. The estate was developed for detached and semi-detached housing fronting Bedford Hill (bottom left view), Abbotswood Road and The Spinney. Battersea Grammar School (seen in this artist's impression and the bottom right photo) was built on the remainder of the site in 1936. It is now Streatham and Clapham High School and has been much extended. See the entry for the school in *Lambeth Architecture 1914-39*.

Spurgeon's Orphanage on **Clapham Road** in Stockwell was a home and school for 500 fatherless boys founded in 1867 by Charles Spurgeon, pastor of the Baptist Metropolitan Tabernacle at Elephant and Castle. It was designed in the Gothic style by James Cubitt and Alfred Wright (seen in the top engraving of 1899). The children lived in house blocks sited around a garden quadrangle (middle photos: 1929). In 1880 orphaned girls were admitted. It included a dining hall (see 1910 interior view), library and infirmary; all built in red brick with stone dressings and blue and yellow diaper and banded brick. The children were evacuated to Surrey at the outbreak of the Second World War, never to return. The site was cleared by the LCC for Stockwell High School in 1960 (see *Lambeth Architecture 1945-65*), replaced by Platanos College in 2012 (bottom right view).

The **Doulton** pottery was established in Lambeth in the 1810s and expanded over the years. In the 1870s the firm decided to build palatial new premises and a tall chimney on the recently completed **Albert Embankment**. Designed by architects Waring, Nicholson and Wilkinson and completed in 1879, the imposing High Victorian-style façades (middle row engraving of 1879 and photo of c1937) graced the river frontage for over 80 years but suffered war damage (bottom left photo of c1950) and were pulled down in c1956. They were replaced by modern office blocks (see *Lambeth Architecture 1945-65*), in turn redeveloped in 2016-17 by the new Corniche residential towers (bottom right). The appreciation of Victorian buildings and their protection by the listing system came too late for what were arguably the most stunning historic landmarks on this stretch of the Thames. Thankfully another fine Doulton building by the same architect, Southbank House, survived this destruction and was listed Grade II in 1974 (see entry on page 73).

Surrey Lodge (see 1881 engraving above) stood on the corner of **Lambeth Road** and Kennington Road. Completed in 1884, it was the grandest block of model tenement blocks in Lambeth. Its frontage block on Lambeth Road was destroyed in 1945 by a V2 rocket which killed 43 people (top right). The surviving rear half stood on Kennington Road/Cosser Street until it was demolished in the 1970s for a student hostel (now the Days Hotel) built in 1981 (right). **Barrett's Bottling Store, 71 Bondway** (bottom row: c1970 and 2015) was a five-storey warehouse built in 1885, used by brewery and mineral water producers. It was demolished in 2016 for the 51-storey New Bondway.

A Few of BRAND & Cº's Specialties

From BRAND & Cº LTᴰ MAYFAIR WORKS
74 to 84 SOUTH LAMBETH ROAD LONDON S.W.

Brand & Co's Mayfair Works at **72-84 South Lambeth Road** opened in 1887, producing fish paste and meat extracts until its closure in the mid 1960s. In 1977 it was replaced by the telecommunications tower, Keybridge House, pictured middle right (see *Lambeth Architecture 1965-99*). The five-storey factory with its projecting clock over the entrance is seen in the middle left view of c1920. In the background are **Coronation Buildings**, four blocks of flats built in c1890 to rehouse residents displaced by the London & South Western Railway's widening of their mainline into Waterloo. The flats (see also top left photo on facing page) were pulled down in 1982 to build 66 South Lambeth Road, a business centre. Bottom left view: the factory in 1967 soon after its closure. The site was redeveloped again in 2016-17 for the Keybridge housing quarter (bottom right).

Guinness Trust Buildings (top right photo) were laid out in 1893 between Glasshouse Street, Vauxhall Walk and the railway viaduct just north of Vauxhall station. The five five-storey tenement blocks of 332 flats were built very close together as is evident from this photo of the arched passage passing under all of the blocks. They were demolished in 1975 to create Spring Gardens (now Vauxhall Pleasure Gardens). Top left photo: **Coronation Buildings** in c1970 (see entry on previous page).

Lambeth is fortunate to retain almost all of its Victorian schools built by the London School Board (see pages 44-49). They are either still in their original use or converted to flats, but a handful were demolished and replaced by new school buildings in the 1960s and 1970s. **Paxton Primary School** (originally **Woodland Road Elementary School**) in Gipsy Hill is pictured left. Designed for a roll of 700 children by T.J. Bailey and opened in 1887, this fine 'triple-decker' was demolished in 1973 and replaced by a single-storey school which in turn was redeveloped as a three-storey school in 2016 (bottom right photo). Two other LSB schools lost in the 1960s were **Ashmole Primary** (by E.R.Robson, built in 1879) on **Ashmole Street** just south of the Oval

and **Johanna Street Primary** in Waterloo. Both were replaced by new two-storey schools opened in 1967-68. Ashmole Primary is featured in *Lambeth Architecture 1965-99*.

The Minet Library, 52 Knatchbull Road was built in 1959 (see *Lambeth Architecture 1945-65* and bottom left photo of c1965) on the site of its 1890 predecessor which had been badly damaged in the Second World War (top right photo: 1940). The original library was designed by George Hubbard (top left photo: 1890), the gift of the local landowner William Minet as a memorial to his wife. It was an imposing Gothic-style design with an octagonal lending library built of red brick with stone dressings topped by a glazed lantern (middle left: interior in c1932. Lambeth Archives occupy the surviving Victorian basement, with a search room on the ground floor, photo below taken in 2017.

The **City & South London Railway** (renamed the Northern line in 1937) opened from King William Street in the City to Stockwell in 1890. It was extended south to Clapham Common in 1900 and then on to Morden via Balham in 1926. Kennington is the only original station building to survive (just over the borough boundary in Southwark). The stations at **Oval** (top photos: 1915 and 2016) and **Stockwell** (bottom views: c1900 and 2016) were of a similar design (both designed by T.P. Figgis) with façades of red brick and stone dressings and magnificent domes which housed the lift equipment. However both were demolished and rebuilt in 1924 (when the lifts were replaced by escalators rendering the domes redundant). Stockwell was demolished and rebuilt again in 1968 as part of the Victoria line extension to Brixton (opened in 1971 - see *Lambeth Architecture 1965-99*) and Oval was remodelled as part of a station upgrade in 1996.

Streatham Town Hall, 244 Streatham High Road was designed by Frederick Wheeler and built in 1888 (top left photo of the frontage block: 1986). The public hall fronting Gleneagle Road was a popular venue for concerts, lectures and public meetings (photo below taken in c1974). Following the closure of the building it was demolished in 1988 and redeveloped as Gleneagle Heights in 2002, middle right view.

Clinton House, 1 Palace Road in Streatham was a detached Queen Anne-style residence built in 1896. It had brick and tile-hung elevations with a pargetted gable and a shell porch hood (photo left: 2009). It was the home of the prolific author of thrillers, mysteries and adventures, Dennis Wheatley (1897-1977) between 1913 and 1922. The house was gutted by fire in 2013 after lying empty for many years and then demolished for new flats called One Palace Road (photo bottom right).

Atholl and Albert Mansions on **South Lambeth Road** are seen in the top left photo taken in 1967 with houses on Radnor Terrace (c1865) and top right, the rear elevation from the junction of Wilcox Road and Rosetta Street in 1965. The six-storey red brick mansion blocks of 1892-95 were built after South Lambeth Road was straightened in c1885 to avoid the double bend of what then became

Old South Lambeth Road. They were all demolished in 1975 to make way for the Mawbey Estate (photo below left). Victoria House and Victoria Mansions on the site opposite survive (see page 112).

The **statue to Henry Fawcett MP** (1833-84) portraying an angel standing over the seated Liberal politician, academic and economist, stood in the centre of **Vauxhall Park** (bottom right photo: c1950) until its removal by Lambeth Council in 1959. Fawcett lived in a large house called The Lawns which stood on the site of the park. Blinded in a shooting accident when he was 25, he was Postmaster General in the 1880s and was a strong supporter of women's rights and the preservation of Epping Forest. The sculpture was by George Tinworth and it was funded by Henry Doulton. It was unveiled by the Archbishop of Canterbury in 1893.

BRIXTON THEATRE
Lessee & Manager   Mr ERNEST STEVENS
General Manager   Mr J. MURRAY HERRIOT

The Brixton Theatre, Brixton Oval was designed by leading theatre architect Frank Matcham with a capacity of over 1,500 seats and opened in September 1896. Its popular pantomime season entertained South Londoners for many years until the theatre was destroyed by a bomb during the Blitz in November 1940. Its foundation stone laid by the renowned actor Sir Henry Irving in 1894 survives in Windrush Square. Its entrance was marked by a tall domed tower between the Ritzy Cinema (1911) and the Tate Library, which is now occupied by a 1990s extension to the Ritzy (middle view). The top two images are from 1900 and c1910, and bottom left in c1945, the bomb damage is evident. The auditorium is seen below in 1906.

BRIXTON THEATRE.   "CINDERELLA,"   6th January, 1906.

Brixton's second theatre, **The Empress** was built on the corner of **Brighton Terrace** and Bernay's Grove in 1898, designed by Wylson and Long (architects of the Tottenham Palace Theatre of 1908, now Grade II listed). The variety theatre and music hall seated 1,260 patrons on three tiers - the stalls, dress circle and gallery, and four boxes, all decorated in the French Renaissance style. Its domed octagonal tower was a local landmark for just 30 years (photo top left: c1900) until it was rebuilt in the Art Deco style in 1931 with a much enlarged capacity of 2,000 as the New Empress (see entry in *Lambeth Architecture 1914-39*). It became a Granada Cinema in 1957 then a bingo hall in 1968.

Its demolition in 1992 was a great architectural loss. It was replaced by a block of three-storey flats (photo right).

The Metropole Theatre (renamed the **Camberwell Empire** in 1906) was designed by Bertie Crewe (1860-1937) and opened in 1894 at the junction of **Coldharbour Lane** and Denmark Hill (bottom left photo c1900). It had a spectacular auditorium and handsome façades. In 1924 it became a cinema with occasional variety shows but was demolished 13 years later and replaced by a purpose-built Odeon Cinema designed by Andrew Mather (see *Lambeth Architecture 1914-39*). This closed in 1975 and was pulled down and replaced by a block of flats and a restaurant (now a Nandos) in 1993 (photo left).

Lambeth Baths stood on the junction of **Kennington Road** and Lambeth Road where Lambeth Towers (1972) is now (top photo - see *Lambeth Architecture 1965-99*). It was designed by A. Hessell Tittman and opened in 1898 offering three swimming pools: Men's First (bottom left photo) and Second Class pools and a Women's pool, a laundry and a slipper baths (photo middle right). It was destroyed by a V2 rocket in January 1945 (bottom right view) along with Surrey Lodge (see page 201). Lambeth planned to build a new swimming pool to replace it but only completed a first phase - Lambeth Slipper Baths and public laundry on Lambeth Walk to the rear, built in 1958 (see *Lambeth Architecture 1945-65*).

BIBLIOGRAPHY AND SOURCES

British History Online - digital library of printed primary and secondary sources of history www.british-history.ac.uk

London Parks & Gardens Trust – Inventory of Historic Spaces - www.londongardensonline.org.uk

Lambeth Landmark – Lambeth Archives Image Collection - www.landmark.lambeth.gov.uk

Lambeth Planning Department Conservation Area Character Appraisals -www.lambeth.gov.uk/planning-and-building-control/building-conservation/conservation-area-profiles-guide

London Borough of Lambeth - List of heritage assets of local architectural or historic interest (Local List)

Stanford Library Map of London (1862) www.mappalondon.com

Ordnance Survey maps at the Lambeth Archives and published on the National Library of Scotland website: www.nls.uk

Lost Hospitals of London www.ezitis.myzen.co.uk

The Diocese of Southwark - record of present and former places of worship - www.southwark.anglican.org

The National Heritage List for England - Historic England - www.historicengland.org.uk/listing/the-list

London Metropolitan Archives - Collage - The London Picture Archive – www.collage.cityoflondon.gov.uk

The Victorian Web - literature, history & culture in the age of Victoria - http://www.victorianweb.org

Survey of London: volumes 23 (Lambeth: South Bank & Vauxhall, 1951) and 26 (Lambeth: Southern Area, 1956)

The Buildings of England - London 2: South - Bridget Cherry & Nikolaus Pevsner - Penguin Books (1994)

The Pubs of North Lambeth - Peter Walker (1989)

A History of Brixton - Alan Piper - published by the Brixton Society (1996)

Buildings of Clapham - The Clapham Society - edited by Alyson Wilson (2000)

Britain's Historic Railway Buildings - A Gazetteer of Structures & Sites - Gordon Biddle - Ian Allan Publishing (2011)

Herne Hill Heritage Trail - revised edition published by the Herne Hill Society (2013)

The Pubs of Dulwich and Herne Hill – published by The Dulwich Society and the Herne Hill Society (2016)

INDEX

Abbeville Road 59

Akerman Road, West Camberwell 125

Albert Embankment 22

Albert Mansions, South Lambeth 207

Albert Square, South Lambeth 114

Aldwinckle, T.W. 34

Alexandra Hotel, Clapham 97

All Saints Church, Clapham Park 171

All Saints Church, North Lambeth 171

All Saints' Church, West Dulwich 163

Angel, North Lambeth 77

Angell Terrace, Brixton 123

Angell Town Literary & Scientific Institute 42

Angell Town, Brixton 124

Archbishop's Park, North Lambeth 53

Archbishop's Place, Brixton 130

Artizans' Laboureres' and General Dwellings Company 141

Ashby Mill School, Brixton 46

Ashmole Primary, Oval 203

Atholl Mansions 206

Atkins Road, Clapham 122

Atlantic Road 71

Bailey, T.J. 44,45,46,47,48,49,144,203

Baines, George & Reginald 167

Baltic House, Brixton 129

Barclay's Bank, Clapham 61

Barclay's Bank, Streatham 63

Barclay's Bank, West Norwood 62

Barker, James 123

Barlow, Peter 188

Barnett, John 172

Barrett's Bottling Store, Vauxhall 201

Barry, Charles 65,69

Barry, E.M. 168

Barry, T. D. 148

Bartleet & Sons 64

Bartleet, W. Gibbs 174

Bazalgette, Joseph 22

Beazley & Burrows 129

Beck, William 186

Bedford Park Hotel, Streatham 105

Bedford Road 126

Beehive Coffee Tavern, Streatham 60

Bell, Charles 179,180

Bell, Stockwell 99

Bentley, John F. 146,161

Bickerdike, Alfred 157

Black Dog, Vauxhall 87

Black Horse, Brixton 92

Blomfield, Arthur 156

Bloom Grove, West Norwood 136

Blore, Edward 170

Bobbin, Clapham 96

Bodley, George 155

Bon Marche Store, Brixton 57

Bonnington Square, Vauxhall 111

Brand & Co's Mayfair Works, South Lambeth 202

Bread & Roses, Clapham 96

Breeds, Arthur Owen 167

Brixton Fire Station 16

Brixton Hill 56

Brixton Police Station 183

Brixton Road 56, 57, 58,71

Brixton Royal Mail Delivery Office 18

Brixton Station Road 71

Brixton Tate Library 28,29

Brixton Theatre 208

Brixton Waterworks 18

Brockwell Park 52

Brooker, J.W. 78

Brunel, Isambard Kingdom 69,182

Bruton, W.M. 88

Bunning, James Bunstone 186

Burton House, West Camberwell 123

Bury, Thomas Talbot 171

Butler, John 14

Calvary Church, South Lambeth 167

Camel & Artichoke, North Lambeth 78

Canterbury Music Hall, North Lambeth 182

Carisbrooke, Tulse Hill 134

Carlton Mansions, Brixton 128

Carlton Mansions, Clapham 121

Causton & Sons Print Works, Stockwell 74

Cavendish Road Police Station 14

Cedars Road, Clapham 120,194

Cedars Terraces, Clapham 119

Centrepoint Soho Vauxhall 111

Charles Edward Brooke School, West Camberwell 48

Chatsworth Baptist Church, West Norwood 177

Chaucer Road 133

Chesterton, Horace 62

Christ Church Hall, Brixton 165

Christ Church, Clapham 148

Christ Church, Streatham 143

Christ Church, West Norwood 152

City & South London Railway 205

City of London Almshouses, Brixton 127

Clapham Common Southside 122

Clapham Dispensary 37

Clapham Fire Station 16

Clapham High Street Station 67

Clapham Library 26

Clapham Manor School 45

Clapham Park, Clapham 122

Clarke, Isaac 145

Claylands Road, South Lambeth 114

Clayton & Bell 175

Cleaver Square, Kennington 107

Clinton House, Streatham 206

Coade lion, Southbank 181

Coade, Eleanor 21,181

Coe, Henry Edward 151

Coldharbour Works, Brixton 75

Collcutt, Thomas 126

Cooper, G. Warren 128

Coronation Buildings, South Lambeth 202

Corpus Christi RC Church, Brixton 161

Cresy, Edward Jnr 16, 17

Crewe, Bertie 209

Crickmay & Son 196

Criffel Avenue, Streatham 140

Crown & Anchor, Brixton 94

Croxted Road Railway Bridge 69

Cruwys, R. 93

Cubitt, James 166,199

Cubitt, Thomas 96,194

Cubitt, Thomas & William 118,122

Currey, Henry 32,187

Curtis Bros Dairy, Streatham 4

Cutts, J.E.K. 160

Darbishire, Henry Astley 110

David Greig, Brixton 54

Dog House, Kennington 81

Dogstar, Brixton 92

Doulton Ceramics, North Lambeth 73

Doulton Ceramics, Embankment 200

Dover House, North Lambeth 59

Dover Mansions, Brixton 128

Drake, Charles 134

Drew, Richard 162,198

Duchy Arms, Kennington 80

Dudley House, West Norwood 134

Dulwich Road, Herne Hill 133

Durand Gardens, Stockwell 117

Durand School, Stockwell 45

Durning Library, Kennington 25

Dyce Drinking Fountain, Streatham 21

Dyce, William 21,150

Eagle Printing Works, Brixton 72

East Brixton Station 184

East Estate, Kennington 109

Edmeston, James 84

Edmonds, Christopher. 156

Edwards, Francis 181

Effra Hall Tavern, Brixton 90

Electric Avenue 55, 56

Elephant & Castle, Vauxhall 84

Elm Park Tavern, Brixton 88

Elm Park, Brixton 130

Elms Crescent, Clapham 122

Elson, B. 96

Empress Theatre, Brixton 209

English Martyrs RC Church, Streatham 164

F. Gough & Co. 104

Fawckner, E. 159

Fawnbrake Avenue, Herne Hill 132

Feathers, Vauxhall 196

Fellowes Prynne, George 162,163

Fentiman Arms, Vauxhall 83

Fentiman Road, South Lambeth 113

Ferndale Road 126

Ferrey, Benjamin 40, 147, 148, 150

Figgis, T.P. 205

Flint Cottage, Streatham 138

Florence, Herne Hill 95

Fowler & Hill 36

Francis & Son, Brixton 54

Francis, F.J. & H. 176

Freemen's Almshouses 127

Freemen's Orphan School, Brixton 186

Friendly Almshouses, Brixton 124

Gardiner, Ralph 134

Gatti's Music Hall, North Lambeth 189

George IV, Brixton 89

George, Ernest 43,60,135,139,158,165,179

Giles, John 152

Gipsy Hill Police Station 14

Gipsy Hill Station 67

Gipsy Hill Tavern, West Norwood 102

Gipsy Hill, West Norwood 136

Glenn, John 107,114

Golden Goose 83

Gothic Lodge, West Norwood 134

Gough, A.D. 174

Grafton Square, Clapham 118

Grand Union, Kennington 82

Great North Wood, West Norwood 101

Green Man, Loughborough Jcn 93

Gresham Almshouses, Brixton 127

Gresham Baptist Chapel 161

Grosvenor, Stockwell 99

Groves, Edward 40

Groveway, Stockwell 117

Guinness Trust Buildings, Vauxhall 203

Habershon, Edward 150

Habershon, William Gilbee 159,173

Hackford Road School 45

Hambly Mansions, Streatham 139

Hammerton's Brewery, Stockwell 189

Hanover Arms, Kennington 80

Hanover Gardens, Oval 107

Haselrigge School, Clapham 47

Haselrigge, Road, Clapham 121

Haslehurst, Edward 31

Hawkshaw, John 69

Heathbrook School, Clapham 46

Helix Road, Brixton 131

Henry Cavendish School, Balham 49

Henry Fawcett Statue, Vauxhall 207

Herne Hill 132

Herne Hill Station 68

Hibbert Almshouses, Clapham 118

Hill Mead School, Brixton 47

Hollis & Son, Kennington 75

Holmewood Gardens, Brixton 131

Holy Trinity Church, North Lambeth 170

Holy Trinity Church, Tulse Hill 148

Hootananny, Brixton 90

Horns Tavern, Kennington 196

Horse & Groom, Streatham 103

Hubbard George 204

Humphreys, James 145

Hungerford Railway Bridge 69

Hungerford Suspension Bridge 182

Hunt, Frederick William 64

Immanuel School, Streatham 43

Jacomb-Hood, Robert 70

Jamm, Brixton 94

Jasper Road, West Norwood 136

Jennings, Josiah George 126

Jewish Orphanage, West Norwood 41

John Tarring & Sons 175

Jolly Gardeners, Vauxhall 86

Josephine Avenue, Brixton 131

Kempe, Charles Eamer 160,178

Kennington Park 50

Kennington PH, Oval 83

Kennington Road School 48

Kennington Road, Kennington 74,107

Kenyon Baptist Chapel, Brixton 159

Killieser, Avenue, Streatham 140

King's Arms, North Lambeth 79

Kingswood School, Norwood 45

Kirkstall Avenue, Streatham 140

Knatchbull Road 123

Knights Hill Tunnel, West Norwood 70

Knowle Road, Brixton 192

Knowles, James T. 37,59,119,120,175

Lambeth Baths, Kennington 210

Lambeth Bridge 188

Lambeth Football Club 4

Lambeth Hospital, Kennington 191

Lambeth New Schools, West Norwood 38

Lambeth Ragged School, Waterloo 39

Lambeth Schools, West Norwood 194

Lambeth Vestry Hall, Kennington 13

Lambeth Walk PH, North Lambeth 77

Lambeth Workhouse, North Lambeth 34

Landor, Brixton 90

Lansdowne Gardens, South Lambeth 115

l'Anson, Edward B. 26,97,121

Lark Hall School, Clapham 44

LCC Weights & Measures Office, Clapham 13

Leander Road, Brixton 131

Leigham Arms, Streatham 103

Leigham Court Estate, Streatham 141

Leigham Court Road, Streatham 138

Lewcock & Grierson 86

Lincoln Tower, Kennington 157

Linton House, Clapham 118

Lion Brewery, South Bank 181

Livesey, Frank & George 76

London & County Bank, West Norwood 62

London Necropolis Railway Terminus, North Lambeth 70

Longfield Hall, West Camberwell 19

Lorn Road, Stockwell 117

Loughborough Hotel, Brixton 93

Loughborough Park 125

Loughborough Park Congregational Chapel 173

Lovejoy, Alfred 109

Lovelace Road, Tulse Hill 135

Low, George 154

Magdalen Hospital 187

Marquis of Lorne, Stockwell 98

Martin, Gertrude 147

Matcham, Frank 182,208

Mawby Arms, Stockwell 98

Mayall Road, Brixton 129

Measures, Harry Bell 111,141

Medora Road, Brixton 130

Messrs Parr & Strong 197

Metropole Theatre, West Camberwell 209

Milkwood Estate, Herne Hill 192

Milkwood Road, Herne Hill 132

Milton Road, Herne Hill 133

Minet Library, West Camberwell 204

Minet, James & William 19,51,123,204

Moore, Temple 178

Mostyn Road Methodist Church, Brixton 175

Muirhead, A.T. 20

Myatt's Fields Park, West Camberwell 51

Myatts Fields, West Camberwell 123

Natwest Bank, Herne Hill 64

Natwest Bank, North Lambeth 62

Natwest Bank, West Norwood 64

Nelson, Thomas Marsh 144

Nevin, William 160

Newton, H.J. 78

Noel Caron Almshouses, South Lambeth 113

North Lambeth Library 30

Norwood Institute, West Norwood 185

Norwood Jewish Orphanage 187

Norwood Road, Herne Hill 133

Norwood Road, West Norwood 59

Oddfellows Hall, Clapham 145

Old Vicarage, Kennington 109

Our Lady of Rosary, Brixton 153

Oval Cricket Ground 20

Oval Gasworks, Kennington 76

Oval Mansions, Oval 112

Oval Station 205

Page, Thomas 65

Palace Road 139

Park Hall Road, West. Norwood 135

Park Hill, Streatham 137

Park Mansions, Vauxhall 111

Parkinson, R. 156

Parris, R. 34

Parsons & Rawlings 57

Paull, H.J. 157

Paxton Hotel, West Norwood 101

Paxton Primary School, Gipsy Hill 203

Peacock, W. 59

Pearsall, Robert 17

Pearson, John Loughborough 41,149

Pendennis Road, Streatham 139

Penfold, John Wornham 6

People's Church, Clapham 160

Peto, Harold 135,139,158,179

Phelps, Arthur J. 153

Pilkington, A.J. 151

Pillar box, Brixton 6

Pineapple, North Lambeth 78

Pite, Arthur Beresford 165

Plough Brewery, Clapham 72

Plumbe, Rowland 141,159

Pratt's Dept Store 190

Prince Consort Lodge, Kennington 108

Prince Regent, Herne Hill 95

Priory Arms, Stockwell 98

Priory Schools, Stockwell 46

Public Convenience, Kennington 20

Purdie, Alfred Edward 164

Queen, Brixton 195

Queen's Head, Vauxhall 86

Queenstown Road 58

Railton Road 58

Railway Bell, West Norwood 102

Railway Tavern, Brixton 93

Railway, Clapham 96

Railway, Streatham 105

Raleigh Gardens, Brixton 129

Raleigh Workshop, Brixton 19

Rathcoole House, Brixton 126

Rectory Gardens, Clapham 121

Redemptorist Monastery, Clapham 146

Reeves, Charles 14,183

Renfrew Road Fire Station 17

Renfrew Road Magistrates Court, Kennington (former) 15

Reynolds, W. Bainbridge 160

Richard Atkins School, Brixton 47

Richborne Terrace, South Lambeth 113

Riggindale Road 139

Roberts, Henry 108

Robins, Eric Cookworthy 153,154

Robson, Edward Robert 44,45,46,49,203

Rogers' Almshouses, Brixton 127

Rogers, William 107,142,171

Rollscourt Avenue, Herne Hill 132

Rose , North Lambeth 87

Rosendale Road 135

Rosendale Road Railway Bridge 69,188

Rosendale Road School 49

Rosendale, West Norwood 101

Ross, Thomas 118

Roupell Park Methodist Church, West Norwood 179

Royal Flour Mills, Embankment 197

Royal Oak, Vauxhall 85

Royal Vauxhall Tavern 84

Scott, George Gilbert (Jnr) 178

Scott, John Oldrid 169

Shaftesbury House, Vauxhall 112

Ship, Kennington 82

Sibella Road, Clapham 121

Smith, George 183

Smith, Sydney R.J. 23, 24, 25, 27, 28, 38

Snell, John 115

Somerleyton Road, Brixton 193

Sorby, Thomas Charles 15

South Bank Lion, Westminster Bridge 21

South Metropolitan Gasworks, Vauxhall 2

South Western Hospital, Stockwell 37,191

Southbank House, Vauxhall 73

Spanish Patriot, North Lambeth 78

Spurgeon's Orphanage, Stockwell 199

St Agnes Church, Kennington 178

St Andrew's & St John's School, North Lambeth 42

St Andrew's Church Hall, Streatham 165

St Andrew's Church, Stockwell 151

St Andrew's Church, Streatham 179

St Anne's Church South Lambeth 156

St Barnabas Church, Stockwell 145

St Cuthbert's Presbyterian Church, Tulse Hill 167

St George's Residences, Brixton 128

St James' Church, Clapham 176

St James's Road, Brixton 193

St James the Apostle Church, West Camberwell 154

St John the Divine Church, North Brixton 1,155

St John the Evangelist Church, Clapham 144

St John's Church, Brixton 147

St John's Crescent, Brixton 124

St John's School, Brixton 40

St Jude's Church, Herne Hill 153

St Leonard's Church, Streatham 150

St Martin-in-the-Fields High School, Tulse Hill 40

St Mary's Church, Clapham 146

St Mary's Gardens, North Lambeth 106

St Mary's School, North Lambeth 43

St Matthew's Church Hall, Brixton 161

St Matthias Church, Tulse Hill 164

St Michael's Church, Stockwell 142

St Olave's House, North Lambeth 110

St Paul's Church, Clapham 156

St Paul's, Brixton 159

St Peter's Church, Clapham 160

St Peter's Church, Kennington 149

St Peter's Church, Streatham 162

St Peter's School/Orphanage & Training College, Kennington 41

St Philip's Church, Kennington 173

St Saviour's Almshouses Chapel, West Norwood 150

St Saviour's Church, Brixton 154

St Saviour's Church, Clapham 175

St Saviour's Church, Herne Hill 42,174

St Stephen's Church, Stockwell 172

St Thomas' Hospital, North Lambeth 32

Stage Door, North Lambeth 79

Stamford Street Estate, North Lambeth 110

Stench pipe, Stockwell 21

Stiff, James 159

Stockwell and North Brixton Dispensary 37

Stockwell Baptist Church, South Lambeth 151

Stockwell Educational Institute 38

Stockwell Park, Stockwell 116

Stockwell School 44

Stockwell Station 205

Stockwell Terrace, Stockwell 116

Stockwell Training College 186

Stone cattle troughs, Streatham & Clapham 21

Streatham Baptist Church, Streatham 158

Streatham Hill Congregational Church & Hall 159,172

Streatham Hill Station 66

Streatham Methodist Church 166,180
Streatham Pumping Station 18
Streatham Tate Library 27
Streatham Town Hall 206
Streatham United Reformed Church 166
Street, George Edmund 1,148,155
Sun, Clapham 97
Sunnyhill Road, Streatham 138
Sunnyhill School, Streatham 49
Surprise, Stockwell 98
Surrey Lodge, Kennington 201
Tarver, E.J. 140
Tate Library, South Lambeth 23
Tea House Theatre, Vauxhall 87
Telegraph, Brixton 88
Telford Avenue, Streatham 140
Teulon, S.S. 42
The Chase, Clapham 120
Thornlaw Road, West Norwood 135
Thornton Road, Clapham 122
Three Stags, Kennington 82
Tillot & Chamberlain 41
Tinworth, George 73,207
Tite, William 168
Tittman, A. Hessell 210
Tommyfield, Kennington 80
Treadwell & Martin 59
Trinity Arms, Brixton 92
Trinity Gardens, Brixton 127
Trinity Presbyterian Church, Clapham 175
Trinity Presbyterian Church, Streatham 158
Trollope, J.E. 30
Tulse Hill Hotel 100
Tulse Hill Station 68
Two Brewers, Clapham 97

Union Road, Clapham 121
Upper Norwood Library 31
Upper Norwood Methodist Church 177
Vauxhall Griffin, Vauxhall 85
Vauxhall Park 51
Vauxhall Station 66
Victoria Mansions, South Lambeth 112
Victoria Rise, Clapham 120
Victoria Tavern, Clapham 99
Vintage House, Vauxhall 74
Vulliamy, Lewis 176
Walcot Square, North Lambeth 106
Walnut Tree Walk School 46
Wandsworth Road 59
Wardell, William 146
Waring, Nicholson & Wilkinson 200
Water Tower, Lambeth Workhouse, North Lambeth 36
Wellington Mills, Waterloo 197
Wellington, North Lambeth 79
Wesleyan Day School, West Norwood 4
Wesleyan Mission Hall, Brixton 160
West Norwood Cemetery 168
West Norwood Cycling Club 4
West Norwood Fire Station 17
West Norwood Library 24
West Norwood Station 184
Westminster Bridge 65
Westminster Business Centre 75
Westmoreland Society School, Tulse Hill 183
Westow House, West Norwood 100
Wheatsheaf Hall, South Lambeth 19

Wheatsheaf, South Lambeth 85
Wheeler & Speed 166
Wheeler, Frederick 206
White Horse, Brixton 88
White House, Oval 107
White Lion, Streatham 104
Wild, James 143
Wilkinson, Fanny 51
Windsor Castle, Brixton 195

Wingfield House, South Lambeth 114
Woodall, Corbet 76
Woodfield Estate, Streatham 198
Wright, Alfred 82,199
Wylson & Long 209
Wynne Road Baptist Church, Brixton 176
Wyvil School 44
Yeates, Alfred 165

Photograph by Jon Newman of the Elephant and Castle at Vauxhall with St George's Wharf in the background in 2006.